EARLY JAPANESE
IMMIGRANTS IN HAWAII

Books by Patsy Sumie Saiki

Sachie, a Daughter of Hawaii
Ganbare, an Example of Japanese Spirit
Japanese Women in Hawaii: the First One Hundred Years

These books can be ordered from the author,
920 Prospect Street, Honolulu, Hawaii 96822

EARLY JAPANESE IMMIGRANTS IN HAWAII

*

by Patsy Sumie Saiki

Japanese Cultural Center of Hawaii

HONOLULU

"Letter to a Daughter" previously published in *Hawaii Herald* and in *Pacific Citizen* (1988). "Just Wait and See" in *Bamboo Ridge* (1978). "Communion" in *The Best of Bamboo Ridge* (1986) and in *Passages to the Dream Shore: Short Stories of Contemporary Hawaii* (1987). "Banzai, Col. Rogers, Sir!" in *Ganbare* (1981). "Graduation" in *Sachie* and in *Asian-Pacific Literature, Vol. I* (1981). "Only One Day," "The Medicine Man," "The Fighter," "Second Son," and "The Sacrifice" in *Sachie* (1977, 1981, 1992). "Two Artists" in *Japanese Women in Hawaii: The First 100 Years* (1985)

Design, composition, and manufacture of this book was through the production services program of the University of Hawaii Press.

Designed by Kenneth Miyamoto

The paper used in this publication meets the minimum requirement of American National Standard Information Sciences—Permanence of Paper for Printed Library Materials ANSI Z.39.48-1984

Distributed by
University of Hawaii Press
Order Department
2840 Kolowalu Street
Honolulu, Hawaii 96822

Contents

v

Preface

M ost Americans are children of immigrants, once or as many as
ten times removed. Each emigrating group has had to cope
with problems in a strange land, problems such as differences in language, religious beliefs, food, and everyday customs and traditions.

A specific group of immigrants welcomed to Hawaii beginning in
1885 was the Japanese, hired to work on sugar plantations. Workers
from other countries imported earlier had found plantation labor
under the hot sun untenable, and had left for other types of livelihood
when their contracts ended. King Kalakaua of Hawaii therefore
encouraged a treaty with Emperor Meiji of Japan to allow Japanese
workers to migrate to Hawaii.

This anthology touches on the lives of these early immigrants. We
share an immigrant woman's unspoken communication with her
Japanese American, English-speaking daughter. We commiserate with
a father who worked for fifteen years to get his son to Hawaii, a son
he has never seen, only to learn that the son can spend only one day
with him.

Another father loses his beloved son to the ocean, and he is made
to realize that for personal reasons he has subjected his wife to a life of
loneliness in Hawaii, away from relatives and friends. Was it worth
the many sacrifices made in emigrating to a new land? A daughter,
born to a Japanese woman and a Caucasian man, tells her Japanese
father that the sacrifice that happened eighteen years ago was because
of the love the mother bore her husband.

We observe how the Japanese members of a community felt—sympathetic but fearful for their livelihood—when a lone immigrant takes on the Territory of Hawaii in a legal battle to the U.S. Supreme Court. We listen in on a communion between a wife and her husband who has been in a coma for several months.

These and other stories, both fiction and nonfiction, are some of the threads from which the fabric of the Japanese society in early Hawaii is woven.

* 1 *

A Letter to a Daughter

The letter was short and simple. Written laboriously on rough lined paper, it had been folded and unfolded again and again, so that the writing was almost illegible. Occasionally there were dark splotches, as if the writer had wet the pencil lead in the mouth.

Namie, mamenaka. Mama sameshiiyo. Tokidoki kake. Hayo modore. Mama genki. Sayonara.

Namie, mamenaka. (Are you well?)

I know you're well. You've never been sick in your fifteen years of life, except the time the measles went around and you caught it at school. *Maa maa,* I can still remember the high fever, and how you went deaf for a week. You scared us . . . you were so limp, so meek and quiet, so wet in your bed from the sweat, even though we changed your clothes every three hours.

Except for that one time, you've always been healthy and strong. I can still see your skinny brown legs flashing up the hill to our vegetable fields when Hanako asked you to get another cabbage to stretch the soup. Or to pull off ten ears of fresh corn to eat after supper, sitting on the verandah watching the Pacific Ocean change from blue to black.

I know you'll be healthy all your life because you've grown up on fruits: apples, oranges, peaches, loquats, bananas, guavas, and berries. You were like a giant yellow-jacket, flitting from one tree to

1

another, eating an apple after polishing it on your dirty dress, sucking the juice of an orange while perched high on a tree, then plucking thimbleberries and popping them into your always busy mouth. Maybe it was lucky we didn't have money for store-bought candy, and you had to make do with fruits and vegetables. Maybe it was lucky your father insisted we leave the sugar plantation and settle on this homestead. Yes, I know you are healthy.

Mama sameshiiyo. (Mama is lonely.)

Oh, how lonely I am, with you in Honolulu attending school. How I wish we had a high school close by, so that you could have stayed here on this island.

You know, Namie, I never wrote a letter until today and I'm fifty-eight years old. I learned because I wanted desperately to keep in touch with you. It was so frustrating, learning the alphabet, the *kata-kana*, which you taught me so patiently last year.

When I was a young child in Japan, I couldn't learn how to read and write too well because the only time girls in our village could attend school was after the rice planting was over or we had completed the harvesting and weeding. It seemed like we always had something to do that prevented my going to school. I loved school, but I couldn't go while my brothers did. Boys were so lucky! But I learned some by listening to my brothers recite from their books. How I loved the stories they read, especially about the peach boy found in a fruit that came bobbing down the stream. For years I believed in Momotaro, just as little children in Hawaii believe in Santa Claus.

I married your father, who was well educated for those days. He emigrated to Hawaii only two months after we were married because there was a special opportunity. There were only twenty young men who left on that ship—the *China Maru*—because the other workers refused to go. They had heard Hawaii was no longer a kingdom and therefore the emigrants didn't have any protection from the government or the plantations. I didn't want your father to go either, under those circumstances, but I had been married only two months and I

2

didn't dare say anything. Besides, your father had his heart set. He said he was getting old, and had no time to waste. He had to earn enough money to buy a plot of land for us, he being the younger brother and not able to inherit anything. I wasn't allowed to go to Kobe, the city from which he left. In fact, I couldn't even go to the train station in Hiroshima City. I worked in the fields as usual, but I think I pulled more vegetables than weeds that day.

From Hawaii he wrote to my father-in-law, his father, instead of to me. Of course he would do that since I was living under his father's roof and eating rice from his father's farm. He had to show respect to his father, and anyway, I couldn't read *kanji*. But I memorized all his letters, so I repeated them to myself all the time. Every time my husband wrote, I was happy. He had not forgotten me, and he would send for me as soon as he had saved enough money for a ticket.

Then fewer letters came. Each night, after the second year, I would pray, "Please, God, let tomorrow be the day my husband sends the money for the ticket and I can go to Hawaii to join him. Please, God . . ." My father-in-law was getting impatient, since a woman can't produce as much as a man but eats almost as much.

That tomorrow came a long four years later. In the meantime I wondered if your father had met another woman in Hawaii, and I would cry silently into my pillow, praying that he hadn't. After all, your father was a tall, good-looking man who carried himself well. We had heard of a farmer from the village on the other side of our mountain who had emigrated to Hawaii and had married a Hawaiian girl. The Hawaiian girl's family owned a lot of land, reaching from the mountain to the sea, this farmer wrote to his parents. What man wouldn't marry a girl with lots of land? So I worried, especially after three years, but not as much as my own mother because if my husband deserted me, I would be sent home to her, no one would marry me, and I would be a disgrace and a burden to my family.

Then the letter and the money finally came! Oh joy! The village chief went to town for the necessary papers which had been prepared earlier, and for the first time I traveled outside our village to a city called Kobe, where one could see many ships. My father-in-law, my father and mother all came on the train with me to see me off. My mother was weeping and beaming at the same time, sad to see me leave and knowing she would never see me again, yet happy that I was finally going to my husband and I hadn't been deserted. My father-in-law stood there, but I knew he was impatient to get back to the farm because he kept pulling his fingers, which he had a habit of doing when he was in a hurry. I sailed on the *Ghyra Maru* in July, when Japan was steaming hot but the inside of the ship was even hotter. There were about 380 of us, and about 350 got sick. They vomited all the time, turned green, and lost so much weight. I was one of the few who went up on deck every day, where we could breathe fresh air. Being so tiny, only 4 feet 11 inches, and so radiantly happy, the sailors did not chase me downstairs, the way they did the men traveling with us. "Get out of our way," they would yell at the men.

Namie, I was shocked when I saw your father. He looked twenty years older than when we had married. He was thinner, his hair was grey, and his body stooped . . . and in only four years! He was forty-eight but he looked like an old, old man to my twenty-eight-year-old eyes. I promised myself I would be the best little wife to him because he had suffered so. He was happy I was there! He took me and my *kori*, my straw container, in a rented horse-and-buggy to a plantation village, and he called out to his friends, "My wife came . . . my wife came . . . come visit us soon!" I'm sure life was easier for him after that, with me cooking, washing clothes, and earning money by working on the plantation too. I was small, but I was young and strong and used to working in the fields.

The other plantation workers told me, "Your husband wanted to save money so badly, he didn't even eat enough. Then he chopped firewood for others, raised and sold vegetables, and did his own washing. It wasn't easy for him, saving money for your ticket." How could I have been thinking about him and a Hawaiian girl? When his only thoughts had been of me? Those four years had been longer for him than for me!

Within a year we moved to this homestead from the plantation, so the children when they came wouldn't have to be told that they must work as laborers on the sugar plantations, else their parents would be evicted. Your father wanted his sons to be farmers on their own land. That was his greatest dream, to own land that he could pass on to all his sons, not just to the eldest. How many times have I seen him sift the rich brown soil through his fingers, so lovingly, so tenderly. He never knew that his sons, except for Toshi, would grow up hating farm work.

Namie, I'm sorry you had such old parents. By the time you started school, your father was sixty-nine and I was forty-nine. The other children in school had parents who were in their twenties, thirties, forties, or some fifties. But you, poor Namie, you had a father who went to school one day and the teacher said, "Why didn't your father come? How come you brought your grandfather?" I remember ever after you refused to have us go to school. You would study hard and obey every rule, so that there would be no need for the teacher to meet with us. And we were so proud of you, always number one in your class, but we were never allowed to go to school to watch you receive a prize. Sometimes I cried. Always I had to wait at home for you to come running up the hill to the kitchen door to shout, "Mama, mama, look, look what I won!" Ah, Namie, you made us so happy . . . you would look at your father . . . when he was still alive . . . then at me, to see which parent's eyes would twinkle first. You would jump to touch the kitchen ceiling, then calmly sit down and gobble a bowl of rice with *tsukemono*, your favorite pickled vegetables. Your father looked twenty years younger then, and I didn't mind not being able to sit with the other parents at school. Maybe it was better that way, for had I seen you receive prize after prize, I would have been so proud, and the other parents would have envied, then hated me.

Tokidoki kake. (Write sometimes.)

Please, a short letter is OK. Don't only write in English to your brothers. Write in *kana*, and have the letter addressed to me. No one has ever written me a letter.

I know you are busy with English and Japanese school, but just a few words. *Okaasan, mamenaka.* Are you well? Look, do you want me to write a letter . . . from you to me? Then I could show this letter to my friends at our monthly church get-togethers. My friends would say, "What a thoughtful daughter you have."

Namie, I am so proud of you, attending high school. You are the first one in our family. Each of your three brothers had hopes of going through high school and even to college, but first your father died, when you were seven, and your eldest brother had to serve as your father. Then, when Toshi was to go, our horse and four cows died, and Toshi insisted he was needed to earn money to buy another horse. He said he would go the following year, but he never did. And of course there was the time two of your brothers contracted diptheria and they were barely kept alive. We were grateful to the doctor for keeping them alive, but we had no money for high school for a long, long time. The doctor was so kind. He allowed us to pay part of his bill in vegetables.

Now it's your turn and finally someone made it. I'm so proud and at the same time so lonely. Also, I'm so tired. Funny, I'm only fifty-eight. My own mother at fifty-eight was healthy, walking to work in the fields every day and carrying a load of firewood on her way back. I was told small skinny women lived long and were healthy. I'm small and skinny. How come I'm so exhausted? I don't have the strength to climb the hill to work in the fields any more.

Hayo modore. (Come back early.)

Of course I don't mean that. You've been away only eight months and seven days. You still have over a whole year to go. Strange, in the past, the days just flew by, and we would say, "What! Another New Year!" Now the days inch by. Two years of not seeing you . . . what a long, long time, although two years is not really that long. I wonder why I feel this way? But I will keep healthy and wait for you. And who knows? Your brothers may get me a ticket to Honolulu some day. For your graduation. After all I have never seen that city. I thought your father would be waiting for me there, when I came from Japan. Instead there was a fat Japanese man in a white suit who took us to a stone building and said, "Okada? You go to Hawaii. Ikeda, you're Maui. Stay over there. Nakamura, you're Maui too. Over there . . ." He made us into little groups and called other men to take us and our *kori* to some small boats where again we were told to go below deck. But that trip took only one night so it wasn't bad, although we tossed this way and that all night long. And your father was waiting, this time, at a place called Hilo. So I never did get to see the city called Honolulu where I had heard there was a queen.

After we moved to this homestead, life wasn't too hard, although after your father died . . . you were in the second grade, I remember . . . I had to load the vegetables on Betani and walk to town each Friday to sell them. I wasn't a good salesman so half the time I had to unload the vegetables on my way home and throw them into this steep gulch. I felt so guilty doing this, throwing those tender ears of corn and those firm cabbages down into the *kukui* grove, but I couldn't give them to people because then they would never buy my vegetables, just wait for me to give them more. And if I took them home, your brothers would say, "How many places did you go to today? Are you sure you weren't just visiting with friends?"

It was three miles to town and I didn't mind the walking, but it was frustrating because Betani insisted on eating the grass growing along the roadside. I couldn't pull him away because he was stronger than I was and real stubborn, but then one day I held a carrot in front of him. He ate it and liked it so much he followed me all the way to town because I held another carrot in front of his nose. Ha! It's so easy to fool an animal.

I had one customer in town, a Mrs. Mita, who was supposed to be rich but who would say, "How are the peaches today?" She would take two of the largest, juiciest, rosiest peaches, eat them and say, "They're tasty, but I still have some apples that I bought from Mr. Otake. I should eat those before I buy more fruit." I used to sell a dozen peaches for a nickel, twenty-five for a dime, and still people would complain. They never knew, these customers, how we had to struggle to pick those ripe peaches every Thursday evening. I had you climb the peach trees with a basket lined with newspapers, and you would pick each ripe, golden peach and place it carefully in the basket. Those ripe peaches bruised so easily . . . they turned from gold to brown quickly. You climbed from slim branch to slimmer branch with that basket and I would call, "There . . . there's one right above your head." You had homework. Sometimes you had a test the next day. Yet you always helped me pick the peaches. Once you fell from a tree and I thought you had broken some bones, since you turned so pale. Besides, you had been up so high. But after a minute or so, while I ran twenty steps to the road to call your brother, then ran twenty steps back to see how you were, you shook your head, picked yourself up, and limped home with all your scratches. Remember? And we didn't have any peaches to sell that Friday. Then that Mrs. Mita says, "Where are your peaches? I might want to buy some peaches today."

You can't imagine what fierce joy it gave me to tell her, "Sorry. No peaches today." I apologized, but I felt triumphant inside. She couldn't have her two free peaches! At that moment, I promised myself to bypass Mrs. Mita's home the following Friday. Not giving her two peaches was worth more than selling her a few vegetables. And you know what? I was so jubilant, so cheery, I sold all my vegetables that day.

Mama genki. (I am healthy.)

The other day a strange thing happened. I started menstruating again. Isn't that funny? To be near sixty and menstruate? I got blood stains on my dress, so I hurriedly washed it so your brother Toshi or Hanako wouldn't find out. I don't know whether it's a disgrace, but at least it's embarrassing, so I'm keeping it a secret. But I'm telling you, Namie, because you're my daughter and I tell you everything, all my secret thoughts. Or at least I want to tell you. I want to share my thoughts, my feelings, with someone. I never had that someone, even when your father was alive.

Sometimes nowadays I'm so tired I stumble when I walk. I lost a lot of weight, and I look haggard. When your brother or your sister-in-law worriedly ask, I say it's because of the heat lately. But it's just as

8

hot for everyone else, so how come I'm the only one to lose weight? And how come my stomach hurts at night? I feel this sharp pain, and I clench my fists and cry a little, but in the morning when I must face your brother and your sister-in-law before they leave for work, I put a smile on my face and force myself to sip a bowl of *miso* soup and nibble at rice and pickled vegetables. It is chiefly at night that this pain twists inside my stomach. It's almost like a baby—in fact I have a large lump that feels like a baby, only it's further down my stomach. Why am I losing so much blood? Sometimes I hold my breath, waiting for the pain to go away, but I pretend everything is OK so that your brother and your sister-in-law will not find out. After all, they will be having a baby some day and will need to save money, so I don't want to burden them with doctor bills. I still remember when your brothers had diptheria, and their education money was all used up.

Namie, did I ever tell you about when you were born? I was standing in the fields spreading fertilizer, since I couldn't crouch to pull weeds. You were already so big in my stomach. All of a sudden I felt you move. I knew you were coming so I called to your father, "The baby! The baby! I'll need hot water." There was no time to run to the policeman's home to borrow the telephone to call the midwife from town. The boys were not home. I had to hold you in, as I walked home slowly, because you wanted to be born in a cabbage patch or in the guava bushes. And when I reached home, the fire under the kettle had started burning, but the water wasn't ready when you were born. So we wiped you with cold water, and it shocked you so that you took a deep breath and yelled. Oh, what an angry cry, a rebellion, that was! And you have been rebelling ever since!

Namie, I'm sorry we were so poor you didn't have a pair of your own shoes until seventh grade. Then, too, you had to wear hand-me-downs from Mrs. Tomita and Mrs. Kondo, who gave me their daughters' dresses in front of everyone else at the church get-togethers. I wanted to refuse those dresses, but some were quite pretty and I knew you needed more than two dresses a year, the way you were growing so tall so fast.

But Namie, we . . . your father and I first, and your brothers and I later . . . were poor but we have never had an unpaid debt. We have never inconvenienced others or cheated them. We have never refused the town people who bought vegetables from other peddlers but who came to us during the Depression years to ask for fruit and vegetables. "When times are good again, we will buy from you. We will remember this kindness," they promised us. They didn't have to say that. We would have shared with them when they were needy.

We have been honest, law-abiding people . . . people you can be proud of. This is the only legacy I can leave you, Namie. I can leave you nothing valuable. The farm is for your brothers. I don't have any jewelry, since neither your father nor I owned a ring or a wristwatch. Your father had a pocket watch which he gave to your oldest brother just before he died

I think of you often, Namie, daughter of my old age, so often nowadays. Your brother picks up the mail once a week, on Fridays, when he goes to sell the vegetables. I wait and wait until he returns. I pretend I'm not anxious, and I force myself to sit quietly on my chair on the verandah, looking for the ten-thousandth time at the Pacific Ocean turning from blue to black, and praying your brother will say, "Why, here's a letter to Mama from Namie! Addressed to you, Mama! A personal letter."

I think of you and miss you most at night, when the pain is now like a knife slashing my insides, and the rags can't stem the flow of blood and I feel drained of strength, of life. And I think, "What if I die before Namie gets back? How will she know I loved her so much? I have never told her, because we Japanese don't talk aloud about love."

The five-sentence letter had never been mailed. But Namie's mother weakly handed Namie the letter when she returned from Honolulu. The cancer operation was too late; the doctor told them it was a matter of days or weeks, not months or years, and her brothers had decided Namie should return immediately. Namie read the letter aloud, then said, "Why, Mama, this is such a good letter." Her mother's face seemed to beam.

It was only a few weeks later that Namie escaped from the house where neighbors worked preparing for her mother's funeral. She climbed the hill past the grove of peach and orange trees, the patches of red thimbleberries, through fields of cabbage and corn and potatoes until she came to the hillside of Easter lilies. Standing among the rows of yellow-tipped white flowers on slender stalks that reached toward the sky, she unfolded the letter and read aloud:

Namie, mamenaka. Mama sameshiiyo. Tokidoki kake. Hayo modore. Mama genki. Sayonara.

Then she whispered, "Mama, this is your gift, your legacy to me. You showed me that we are never too old to learn. We are always to keep growing. Thank you for this letter. I will treasure this more than anything else you could have given me. And Mama, *genki de neh?* I will be healthy too. And, some nights, I will reach for the sky, and could you please touch me and comfort me, the way you always did. Even from up there, will you please keep loving me and sharing your strength with me? Mama, *sayonara . . .*"

* 2 *

Only One Day

"Come, Sachie, let's check the fences. We don't want our cows going into Gouveia's land and eating his grass," her father said one Saturday. "And don't forget the *obento*. Make two rice balls for me." He tucked his flute into his back pocket, picked up his box of tools containing hammer and fence nails, and left.

Sachie was happy. Her father could have gone any day of the week to mend the fences. That meant he wanted to spend some time with her, unlike Sachie's mother who preferred to work alone.

Why was her mother so stern? She was kind, she was gentle, she was friendly, but as soon as love seemed to flow from her, she cut it off. She would not let herself love anyone too much. Sachie did not have the same feeling for her mother that she had for her father.

The *obento*! Never mind about her mother for now. She had a job to do. Her father would be waiting for her. Sachie got up, washed her hands, sprinkled salt on them, and made four quite triangular balls of rice, each with a red pickled plum in it. She put these in a box, together with some dried fish and slices of pickled turnips.

Sachie ran west to the row of eucalyptus trees which separated their land from Gouveia's property. She found her father walking along the path which ran parallel to the fence, his right shoulder slanted by the weight of the tool box. Sachie remembered he was seventy; she didn't think she would ever live to be sixty or even fifty.

"I'll carry the box," Sachie offered.

"Never mind," her father answered. "It's not heavy."

13

"I'll take it," she insisted, pulling it from him and running ahead to pick a ripe guava. She was barefooted, and her long brown arms were uncovered. Alternately she ran ahead, then lagged behind, teasing a bee, picking a ripe purple *lilikoi,* or chasing a Monarch butterfly. After a while she fell in step with her father.

"Father, I wish I weren't Japanese."

"I thought you were an American, not Japanese."

"You know what I mean. And why wasn't I born to a doctor or lawyer or teacher, instead of to a farmer?"

"You haven't been happy with us?"

"Oh, I love you and the family, Father. It's just that I had to spend one-fourth of my life stuck on this farm. I wish I were twenty-one, out of college, and able to go anywhere in this world . . . And I wish I weren't Japanese."

"Why?"

"Look at me. Straight black hair . . . stiff hair, like the horse's tail. Slant eyes, when I want round eyes. And I'm so black."

"You're not black . . . you're just tanned . . ."

"I'm not tanned. I'm black. Do you know what the kids call me? Charcoal. That's because I'm dark, and then because we make charcoal to sell."

"What's wrong with making charcoal to sell? People buy all we can make. They even put in their orders months in advance."

"Also, I'm so tall. That's your fault, Father, because I take after you. Hanako is small, like Mother. I hate it when Mother says, *"Einyobo konyobo"* . . . a beautiful woman is small and dainty."

"Do you believe that saying?"

"And that other saying . . . *iro shiro wa hichinan kakusu* . . . a fair complexion hides seven faults. Hanako is small and fair, and I'm tall and dark. I have nothing going for me."

"Ah, but aren't you one of the smartest girls in your grade at school?"

"Are you kidding? Even that's against me. . . . But there's one boy who likes me, I think. It's Jerry Higa."

"Well, aren't you lucky! He's such a courteous, friendly boy. And

14

with a sense of humor . . . he's always making people laugh. Have you noticed, when he's around, all the other boys and girls become friendly and courteous? He's such a good influence."

"And another thing . . . my teacher laughed when she found out you were seventy years old. She must have told the other teachers, because the librarian asked me if my father was really seventy."

"Hummm . . ."

"Someone said you're pretty old to have a child my age. My friends' fathers are all younger than forty-five."

"Hummm . . ."

"How come you're so old?"

"We grow older every day. I guess I was born too soon."

"Don't joke about it, Father. Most people seventy are dead."

"I don't think so. My older brother in Japan is still alive. Even my mother died only a few years ago. I think I can outwalk half your friends' fathers."

"My teacher said you were fifty-five or fifty-six when I was born."

"What's wrong with being a father at fifty-six? Especially to a girl like you?"

"Stop joking. You're always joking. Are you glad you came to Hawaii?"

"Of course!"

"My teacher says all foreigners should be glad they came to Hawaii . . . or to America . . ."

"She's right. Her ancestors must have been very glad."

"She said Japan doesn't have much level land, mostly mountains, and the people are poor. They don't have enough to eat. Did you have enough to eat, Father? In Japan?" She bit into another guava.

"Don't eat too many guavas. You'll get appendicitis. Then we'll have to take you to the hospital and open you up. Take out your appendix."

"Did you have enough to eat? In Japan?"

Her father tested the tautness of fence wire, sighed, and said, almost as if to himself, "I had enough to eat, but I was the extra person, being the younger brother. My older brother, who owned the land after my father died, had to share the rice with his wife, three children, my mother and me. When I got married, there was still another mouth with whom to share the rice. It was unfair to my brother, since there was so little land, so when I found out about Hawaii, I decided to come here. I wanted to earn money to buy my own farm in Japan."

He gazed at the green hills that made up part of his fifty acres. "They needed workers in Hawaii. A man came from Tokyo to act as interpreter. He came with a white man in a white suit. It was the first time I had seen a white man or a white suit or blue eyes. I was scared of him, he was so huge and hairy . . . like a monkey . . . but he wanted to shake hands with us. Maybe that's why I decided to come with my friends. The white man's handshake was firm, but so friendly. And his hands were so clean, while ours were dirty. But he insisted on shaking hands anyway."

Her father said proudly, "The interpreter said this white man wanted workers from Hiroshima prefecture. The man didn't want workers from Tokyo. Anyone knows people from Hiroshima are hard workers. Even the white man from across the sea seemed to know that."

"Must have been scary, coming across the ocean to a new country," Sachie said.

"Yes, it was. But when I came, they said I was a free immigrant. That meant I didn't have to work for the plantation if I didn't want to. Of course there was no place else to work, since I didn't understand the language, so I went to work on a plantation. We were paid $12 a month."

"Only $12 a month? That's too little!"

"Oh, but remember, this was in 1895. Those who came earlier worked for $4 a month. Twelve hours a day, six days a week."

"That's not fair."

"Oh, it was fair. We came because we wanted to. We were provided a place to sleep in. Things were cheaper then. . . . Did I tell you I came on the *China Maru*? There were only twenty of us, that time in 1895, and we all became good friends during that one month on the ship. We called the ship *Nippon Maru* because in Japan we had

16

been trained to hate the Chinese. There was a war between Japan and China that year. Of course it was hard to hate the Chinese because I had never seen one in my life until I came to Hawaii. And when I came to Hawaii, I found the Chinese were like my brothers. . . . We kind of looked alike, we could read each other's written language, we ate about the same kind of food, . . . and together we disliked the Portuguese *luna*s and the *haole*s, because they were our bosses."

"What about the Hawaiians?"

"We didn't see many Hawaiians, except for the Akinas. The Hawaiians didn't work on the plantations. They worked on the ranches . . . their own or on Parker Ranch. But they hated the *haole*s more than anyone else, because the *haole*s were taking the land away from them."

"Oh, that was the time of the revolution? Queen Liliuokalani?"

"That came a few years later. I came in 1895. In 1897, over one thousand Japanese came to work in Hawaii, but the government wouldn't let them land. The American government, that is. Poor workers . . . they spent all their life savings getting ready to come to a place they didn't want to come to, and then the new land didn't want them. I told you about this, didn't I?"

"Yes. Mother came in 1899, you said."

" 'Yes. There were close to four hundred people on the ship she came on, and this was July . . . mid-July. You can imagine how hot and stuffy the bunks and cabins must have been. Poor Mother! That was a popular year for immigrants. Would you believe over 25,000 Japanese immigrants came to Hawaii that one year? More than any other year . . ."

They reached the large cypress tree at the top of the hill overlooking most of the farm land. Her father sat down and leaned against the rough trunk of the tree. Below them were green fields. In the pasture, Charlie, the white horse, and Betani, the reddish one, nibbled daintily. In one of the fields, Sachie could see her mother, a white cloth towel around her head to keep the sun out, and blue denim on the rest of her. She was bent over the cabbage rows, slowly going from one plant to another, occasionally straightening up and pounding her shoulders.

"Sachie, when you see an old immigrant, you should honor and respect him, because it's not easy to go to another country. The food is different, the language is different, and you can't catch a bus or train and go home when you feel you can't stand it one day longer. To be so far away from home, and not have the money to return. And knowing you wouldn't be welcome even if you did return, if you couldn't settle on your own farm."

He sat down in the shade, putting his flute to one side, and closed his eyes. "We were miserable, miserable," he recollected. "I think it was chiefly because we couldn't understand what our bosses wanted. All we knew, that first year, is what the interpreter said. Even when the *luna*s scolded us or beat us, we didn't know what it was for. Once a *luna* beat Honda, who was digging a ditch. Honda dug faster and faster, and the *luna* yelled at him and even threw dirt and rocks at him. Later we found out he wanted Honda to stop digging, to do something else.

"We all wanted to go back to Japan so badly. We talked of nothing else except the farms we were going to buy when we got home. But of course it was hard, saving money. Finally, when I reached Kakela, I decided to have your mother come. Then, when Toki was born, then Haruo, well, we sort of changed our minds about going back . . .

"On the plantation, we slept in a small room, eight of us. My space was a three-by-six mat. Every time I yawned and forgot, I hit Tanaka in the face, and he would punch me. We had to sleep straight, like in a coffin. And Honda! Honda was always yelling in his sleep because the *luna* would beat him all the time. Honda would scare us, yelling in the middle of the night, and bowing and apologizing. How many times we had to wake him up. Poor Honda!"

"What happened to him?"

"Honda? The last we heard, he was in Honolulu. They say his son is in a university there. Imagine, Honda's son going to a university! How proud Honda must be. He was always black and blue, because the *luna* liked to pick on him. Some day, Honda used to say, some day he was going to kill the *luna*."

"Did he?"

"Did he what?"

"Kill the *luna*."

"Honda couldn't even kill a chicken. Although he was a good cook. And that's the funny part. Honda started learning English, and then, since he was a good cook, the big boss, the one who bosses even the *luna*s, asked Honda to be his cook. After that, the *luna* couldn't do anything to Honda, even though Honda acted sassy to him. Honda said once he spit on that *luna*'s food before serving him, to pay for all the beatings he had gotten. But I don't believe that.

"The big boss took good care of Honda; in fact, I think he is paying for Honda's son's education. That's the thing you can't understand about the white people. The good ones are so good, and the mean ones are so mean. Take Mr. Scott, the big boss. He's a really good man. Then take Bakka-man. He's hurt so many families in Fraserville. Thank heavens the people in Kakela are smarter, and don't get taken in by him."

He sat up to look at Sachie, seemed satisfied, then said, "Let's eat. What did you bring for lunch?"

After their rice balls, dried fish, and pickled turnips, he took his flute and began playing a tune he loved. The high sharp notes pierced the clear air over the pasture and reached the fields below.

At the sound of the flute, her mother straightened and looked toward the hills. Then, slowly, she bent down again to her work. Her father saw the movement, even at that distance. He put the flute aside and said, "Come, let's see if we can help your mother."

"But you just started playing," Sachie protested. She wanted to lie under the cypress tree, listening to her father's music, listening to him talk.

But her father, without another word, picked up his tool box and flute and walked down to the vegetable fields.

Her mother was bent over a cabbage. She would peer between the leaves of a loosely formed cabbage, turn over a leaf, pick up a worm, and rip it in two. Somehow she knew just where the worm would be.

"Sachie, go and gather the dried horse manure. The pile in the shed is low. If we leave the manure out too long, it won't be any good."

This was terrible. Sachie had thought her mother would ask her to pick off the cabbage worms. She hated killing cabbage butterflies, since they looked so pretty in the air and as they fanned themselves on a cabbage leaf. She hated even worse finding the green worms and ripping them in two. Yet that had to be done, or there would be few cabbages worth selling. But collecting manure . . . this was the worst job on the farm. The menfolk did not have to do it. Only women and girls were given such dirty jobs.

"I'm helping Father check the fences," Sachie said.

"Your father can check the fences without you," her mother answered. She went back to the cabbages.

"Go ahead, Sachie. See how much you can get. We sure can use that manure," her father said.

As Sachie slowly made her way to the shed where the wheelbarrow, shovels, and manure were kept, she thought, "Mother is so unfair. She makes me do all the dirty jobs. My brothers don't have to do smelly jobs like this." Always, it seemed, the boys were favored.

"Don't eat until the boys start," her mother would say. Then, when she could eat, she had to eat the scorched rice first.

"Clean up your bowl," her mother said. "Do you think we have rice to waste? Every grain came from Japan, thousands of miles away. Do you think the farmers raised this rice and sent it over that ocean for you to give to the pig? You musn't waste even a grain of rice."

But to her brothers, her mother would say, "Leave some rice in the bowl. It shows you can waste rice if you want to. We have to fool the gods into thinking we are rich and can waste rice. Even the gods like rich people."

It was the same with the bath. Always, the boys and her father would have to finish bathing before Sachie could scrub herself and soak in the square wooden tub of steaming water.

Sachie got the wheelbarrow, a shovel with a short handle, and some burlap bags. The day was warm, and the task not too unpleasant. The manure was dry and light, like tufts of dried grass. If no one knew, she thought, I wouldn't mind doing this. But if my friends found out, they would call me "Manure Girl" in addition to "Charcoal." Why can't Mother buy fertilizer, like the other farmers, she fumed.

"My, such industriousness. Why do you work so angrily?"

She had not even heard her father coming. "I don't understand Mother. She doesn't like me, the way she does things only for Haruo and Toki. Always it is Haruo and Toki, not Hanako and me. Just because they're boys."

"Nonsense, Sachie, of course your mother loves you. Maybe even the most, since you're our youngest."

"She's not fair."

"Maybe it seems that way to you. After all, she was raised in Japan and she wants to raise you the way she was brought up. She sees the way young people are acting nowadays, and she's afraid you children will be like that too."

"Like what?"

"Well, like . . . not respecting your parents. Some young people are so rude to their parents. They don't speak to their parents just because the parents can't speak good English. But the parents are good in Japanese, where the young ones are good in English. What makes the young ones better than the parents?"

"This is America. This is Hawaii. The parents should learn English. How long have you been in Hawaii, Father? Over thirty years? Isn't that long enough to learn a language?"

"Sachie, Sachie, it's not that simple. It's so hard to learn English. English goes *balabalabala* . . . By the time your brother was six, he was already our interpreter."

"I don't think you even tried to learn English."

"Getting food in our mouths then was more important than learning English, Sachie. Some day, when you're older, and you want to learn another language . . . German or French or even Chinese . . . you'll find how hard it is."

"Mother still makes me mad. Always picking on me. Just because I'm not more like Hanako. But I don't want to be like Hanako. She has no guts. She's sweet just because everyone says she's sweet, and now she's a goody-goody."

21

"Sachie, you know you don't mean that. Are you jealous because Hanako's hair is curly, she's fair, her eyelashes are long, and her eyes are round?"

Sachie stopped shoveling manure into the burlap bag. "Maybe," she finally admitted.

"Sachie, try to understand your mother. She's had such a hard life. Living in Japan with my mother, my brother, and his wife for so many years, and losing a son . . ."

"What do you mean, losing a son?"

"We had a son in Japan, Sachie . . ."

"Had? We had a brother in Japan? How come no one ever said anything about this? How can you treat me like that, not even telling me about my own brother?"

"There wasn't any use in telling you about him. By the time you were born, he was dead. Your mother never talks about him . . . never even mentions his name . . . although I notice she leaves food in the altar for him on his birthday. And I never think of him if I can . . ."

"Tell me about him. What was his name? How old was he when he died? Where is he buried?"

"Yoshio. Eighteen. In Japan. He died all alone, even though my older brother tried to be good to him. But he had tuberculosis, you see, and there was no cure for tuberculosis in those days. My brother and his wife were afraid for their own children . . . afraid of their catching it . . ."

"Why did you send him to Japan?"

"We didn't. He was born in Japan, after I came to Hawaii, and before your mother came. I had a hard time saving money for him to come to Hawaii. But when I did get the money, when he was about fifteen, he caught pink-eyes on the ship."

"What is pink-eyes?"

"I don't know what the English word for that is. But the immigration people said anyone with pink-eyes could not remain in Hawaii. It was the law. But they must have felt sorry, for they let him off the ship for one day. For that I am grateful."

"What did you do?"

"We walked. And walked. And walked. I don't know where we walked. It's a wonder we found our way back to the ship. Yoshio cried, not because he had to go back to Japan but because he had expected to see his mother again. He wouldn't believe she lived on another island, and he kept saying, 'If we walked real fast, could we reach home and be back in time?' He was about your age, but he looked and acted younger, much younger. And so pale. Even fifteen days cooped up on that boat had made him thin and pale."

He picked some blue flowers from a weed and made a tiny bouquet. "Then, on the way back to Japan, he caught tuberculosis from someone who also hadn't been allowed to land. Three years after that he died, at eighteen, when a person should be at the happiest stage of his life. He died all alone in a small shack my brother built for him in a corner of the land where no one could see him. I understand that even when they took him three meals a day, they didn't stay to talk to him. The poor boy . . . we tried to do good for him by bringing him to Hawaii, and instead we killed him, for he would have been healthy otherwise. The pink-eyes, the tuberculosis—they were diseases caught on the ship, and we never dreamed this could happen!"

He threw the flowers, one by one, at his feet, and made a little mound of them with his shoes. "Your mother was waiting for us at the pier at Konohina. I could see her from the interisland boat. She kept coming so close to the water, I thought she would fall in. She looked and looked for Yoshio, but she hadn't seen him for over ten years so she didn't know what he looked like. He had been only four when she had left him in Japan. Only four . . . just about able to understand. She said she couldn't bear to part with him at the train station, so they had him go to a candy store with his cousin. I understand my older brother grumbled about her leaving this small child for them to support, but I just didn't have enough money for the passage of two people then.

"Can you imagine that little child waiting and waiting and waiting for his mother to come home? How many times he must have asked, 'Where's Mommy? When is she coming home?' Even if my brother's family said, 'She's in Hawaii' what's Hawaii to a four- or five-year-old? That poor, poor child . . . who grew up without a real family of his own! He must have said, 'Finally I'll be with my mother again. I'll see my father, and I have two brothers.' How happy he must have been when he boarded that boat. He didn't know then it would be the cause of his death."

A cloud passed over the sun and darkened the field for a moment. Her father looked at the cloud, and then the cloud passed and the sun was too bright for his eyes for he had tears in them.

"I still remember that day, Sachie. Your mother wouldn't even cry. When we got home to Kakela, she went to the fields and dug the ground with a pick until midnight. I tried to get her to come home . . . I told her we would save more money and send for him again, but she wouldn't even speak to me. She knew we would never be able to save that much extra money again, and a new law was going to be passed soon so that Japanese immigrants wouldn't be allowed to come to Hawaii.

"Only once she asked, 'If they let him off the boat, why didn't you sneak him into the interisland boat and bring him home? We could have hidden him in the woods. We could have built him a small house. The government wouldn't have minded. After all, it was only pink-eyes. All I had to do was wash his eyes with boric acid. It wasn't as if he had tuberculosis. Why didn't you bring him back?'

"But then she said, 'What am I saying? No, no, we couldn't do that. After all, we're Japanese. We're law-abiding people!' "

Sachie could imagine her mother digging in the fields. Even today, when she was angry, she would dig in the garden instead of slamming doors or crying.

"Ah, Sachie, how hard it was to say goodby to my son and know that I would never see him again. Better if I had never seen him at all . . . better not to know what my son looked like than to remember him as he walked back into that ship, so small . . . so scared . . . with the small amount of money I was able to borrow from a hotel man. He was only fifteen, after all. He looked so lost on that ship, with just a few others that the immigration officers wouldn't allow to remain. Only one day in Hawaii, and another half a month on that rolling, smelly prison of a ship." Her father looked older, more stooped. "When Yoshio died, part of your mother died too. Now she doesn't want to love anyone too deeply, for fear the gods will take that person too. She's so afraid.

"So when she seems to ignore you, Sachie, and tries not to show love, remember, it must be because she loves you so much she doesn't want the gods to know it."

He looked at the bags of manure Sachie had collected and said, "Here, let me take the wheelbarrow to the shed for you. I'm old, but I can do that much."

But already her mother's training was a part of her, and Sachie knew she couldn't allow her father to do that. So she said, "No, father, I can do this by myself. You go check the fences. And don't eat too many guavas. You might get appendicitis."

Her father smiled. Sachie was proud of the look on his face.

* 3 *

The Medicine Man

"*O chini no kusuriyasan!* The medicine man! The medicine man is coming!"

Always, in December, the medicine man came, ringing a distinctive bell from his ancient Ford. He sold not only medicine; he shared news and gossip from the various communities and islands. He had a phenomenal memory and was a walking encyclopedia of both Japan and Hawaii.

Ossan had *jintan,* a tiny pellet which was supposed to be good for any minor ailment and to keep the mouth smelling sweet. Another was *gotosan,* a yellowish powder wrapped in a square of waxed paper and which was guaranteed to lower a fever. Then there was *koyaku,* an ointment in a half clam shell, which was used for boils and other skin infections. *Mikkasan* was for before and after childbirth; *akadama,* a tiny red pellet, for diarrhea; *sokkoshi,* a plaster for headaches; and *kumanoi,* a vile smelling and bitter tasting paste presumably made from the liver of a bear, for stomachaches.

Of course the best known, and one a family with children would never be without, was *mushikudashi. Mushi,* or worms, could be blamed for any number of things. If children whined, with eyes red and puffy, they had *mushi,* tiny white pinworms. If children were finicky about their food, they had *mushi,* a long earthworm that had somehow bred or made its way into the intestines. If childen were temperamental or looked or acted in any way different from their usual selves, they were told they had *mushi,* and were given *mushikudashi,* which meant, literally, "a washing down of worms."

Ossan trusted all people so long as they were Japanese. He left his medicine, whatever was requested, and six months later people paid him for whatever they had used. He replenished their supply and another six months later was back again. Whenever anyone moved, which was very seldom, he was sure to leave his name and address or his money for the medicine man. To cheat the medicine man was unthinkable! So today, when the familiar tinkle came before the black Ford itself, both Sachie and her mother hurried out to greet tired, dusty Ossan. But although the Ford and the bell were the same, the man was a stranger.

"Oh, you must be Himeno-san," he called out. "I'm Nishida, and I'm taking Tanaka-san's place because he's elderly and can't work at this job anymore. The driving around the different islands was too much. You know how bad the roads are. So bumpy . . . so dusty . . ."

He could not miss the disappointment in the faces, so he added, "I knew this was the Himeno farm because Tanaka-san told me you had the most beautiful garden in Kakela. My, you have a lovely view, being on a hilltop like this. What mountain is that?"

"That's Kohala Mountains, and that one is Mauna Kea. And do you see that mass of black over there? That's the island of Maui."

"*Maa*, imagine being able to see that far. The air is so clear here . . . And the smell . . . why, isn't that the rare three-needle Japanese pine?"

"Yes," Sachie's mother said proudly. "And look, do you know what kind of tree this is?"

"A tea bush! My goodness, a teabush in Hawaii! Why, just seeing and smelling this tea bush takes me back to my home village in Shizuoka, where we raise tea on every hillside. And do you know, we used to raise such fragrant tea, but we had to drink bitter tea made from tough leaves that we couldn't sell, and from the small stems? Only at New Year's could we drink tea made from the fragrant new leaves . . ."

Somehow this admission endeared the new medicine man to Sachie's mother, for she invited Nishida-san to stay the night and to tell them what was happening in the world outside their homestead community.

That night they all sat in the living room to talk. Ossan told them about the things he had seen and heard on his trips.

"Did you know that an Old People's Home is going to be built in Honolulu for the old and needy? There are some old Japanese men on welfare and some in the Charity Hospital, and when the Japanese Care Home is built, such cases can be taken care of there."

"What happened to the children of these old people? Why aren't they taking care of their parents?"

"These men are single men. They have no one to turn to."

"How sad . . . I used to envy them, the way they lived," Sachie's father confessed. "They gambled. They had warm clothes in winter. They encouraged and pleaded with other men's wives to cheat on their husbands, and they were always laughing and having a good time. Now they must depend on strangers to take care of them."

"Yes, it's sad," the medicine man agreed. "Also, did you know some Japanese who served in World War I had been promised citizenship and even given papers, but the Territory refuses to recognize this citizenship? All the other races . . . except the Asians . . . got their citizenship. The Japanese cannot be naturalized. We have been good citizens, obeying all laws, paying all taxes, but we can't ever be naturalized as Americans, even though we've lived here over fifty years."

"Don't give up hope, Nishida-san. The government could still change when they see what good people we are. Our childen are citizens, anyway, and that's what's important. We have only a few more years to live, but our children have a lifetime ahead of them."

"Did you know our children are dual citizens? Citizens of Japan and citizens of the United States? If you sent your sons to Japan, they could be conscripted into the Japanese army."

Sachie's father laughed. "There's no fear of that, at least. We don't have money to go to Hilo, let alone Honolulu or Japan."

"The Japanese children in the English schools have done well," the medicine man explained. "In fact, the plantations don't want Japanese children to have too much education. If the children graduate from high school, they may not want to work on the plantation, at least in the fields."

"That may be true of some plantations, but we have a plantation boss in Fraserville . . . a Mr. Scott . . . who used to send Japanese children to Hilo to finish high school. Sometimes even to Honolulu, to enter college!"

"Well, he's a rare one. Most plantation bosses don't want more than eighth grade education for their workers. Of course, right now, with this depression, they have nothing to worry about. There are four or five people for every job available. You're lucky, Mr. Himeno. You have a farm. People in the towns aren't eating too well, you know. But you, you have all the vegetables you need."

"Yes. But of course we have to work hard . . . months . . . to raise any vegetable. Now fruit trees, like orange, apple, peach, and persimmon . . . that's another matter. They just bear fruit from year to year."

"How many acres do you have?"

"Fifty."

"Fifty! And your own cows, so that you have all the milk you need."

"Only four cows . . ."

"How lucky you are. And I heard you've been sharing your vegetables and fruits with needy families in town."

"Oh, that's nothing. People don't have the money to buy vegetables because they don't have jobs now. They've been customers of ours in the past, so where I can help, I try to help."

"Everywhere, people have been praising you. They hold you in such high respect. You care about people, and you do something to help."

"The gods have been kind to me. See, Sachie, being on a farm is not all that bad."

Sachie had heard this many times, so she hastened to her room, but left the door open so she could hear what was being said.

"Tomorrow morning, you'll be going to see the Itoga family, about a quarter mile up the road. Ah, such a sad family. You mustn't act surprised if you see anything different."

"What do you mean, different?" Sachie was glad Ossan asked the question because she was curious too. She had never thought of the Itoga family as being sad or different from other Kakela families.

"The two older children are *hapa,* half Japanese and half white," her mother explained. "But it wasn't any of the family's fault," she hastened to add. "Mrs. Itoga is a good woman who would die for her husband. It all happened because Mr. Itoga became tubercular."

"Did whatever happened happen while he was in the hospital?"

"No, when Mr. Itoga became ill, Mrs. Itoga had to go to work, and the only job she could get was as a maid in a white man's home. She became a maid so that she could take home soup and eggs and meat for her husband—food the white man was going to throw away anyway. Mrs. Itoga was a tiny, beautiful woman—fair and fragile—and could have lasted working on a sugar plantation for only a few months, maybe. What sacrifices she must have made, what agony she must have suffered, for her husband's sake. She had a baby, and it had such blue blue eyes. The white man wanted her and the baby girl and husband to leave right away, because he knew what the community would say. But the white man's wife insisted Mrs. Itoga and her husband and baby girl stay until Mr. Itoga could get a job. That shows how kind she was, this white woman, how she really cared about the Itogas, even though they were Japanese laborers and people gossiped behind her back.

"But about two years later, Mrs. Itoga had another baby, a boy this time, and again with blue blue eyes. The woman gave Mrs. Itoga money and told her to take her husband to a homestead in Kakela, where Mr. Itoga could have clean air, fresh fruits and vegetables. The Japanese families here helped them to get settled, just as they helped me, and now Mr. Itoga is much better and can work on the farm a little. They've been here fifteen years, I think."

"Did the white man's wife send the Itogas away because she was afraid the Itogas might try to claim an inheritance through the boy? After all, they didn't send the Itogas away when they had a girl."

31

"No, no, that's not the way we heard it. We understood the white man's wife was rather sickly and childless, and she was becoming so attached to the children, she sent them away before she found she couldn't give them up."

"What a good, kind woman she was," the medicine man murmured. "Like a Japanese woman, wasn't she? Keeping Mrs. Itoga even after the first baby was born . . ."

"Wasn't she, though. That's what puzzles us about the white man. The good ones are so good."

"It's too bad the husband couldn't resist temptation. Yet I can't say I blame him, for any Japanese man would have done the same thing if he had a beautiful young maid in his house and his wife was sickly. Don't you think so?"

"Well, not all Japanese men, but many, yes. Even here, in the islands, we have Japanese men who try to steal the Japanese women from their husbands, just because they don't want to pay or can't pay passage money for a wife from Japan. So I guess men are men no matter what country they come from."

"So some of the white men are good men!"

"Oh, yes. You take Mr. Scott, the head boss of the plantation. He's like a father to the people, even to us in Kakela, though we're not plantation workers. When someone is ill, he can go to the plantation doctor for free. When a boy from Kakela broke his arm . . . he fell from a tree . . . Mr. Scott told the hospital not to charge the family anything . He's that good."

"But there's one man, a man we call Bakka-man, who's a pest," Sachie's mother broke in. "He's made several girls pregnant. He hires them as maids and promises them and their parents all kinds of things."

"Why doesn't someone report him to this Mr. Scott?"

"They did, but nothing happened. I don't know if it's true because we don't associate with plantation white men, but someone told us Mr. Scott's sister was Bakka-man's wife, and she ran away with another man. And that's why Bakka-man is like that. He's ashamed so he tries to show he can get any girl he wants. They say Mr. Scott doesn't fire Bakka-man because he understands Bakka-man's hurt and shame, and he feels guilty about his sister running away from her husband."

Sachie shivered in anticipation. What a story she had for the gang who waited for the school bus under the roseapple tree. Then she remembered Ayako and Shigeo, with their sparkling blue eyes, who were part of the gang. All this information couldn't be shared.

"Grow up," she told herself. "Can't you keep anything secret?" Then she recalled what the medicine man had said to her father, "Everywhere people praise you. They hold you in such high respect." Was her father a somebody, after all? Even stuck on a farm? Father cares about people . . . he cares . . . was that the secret to being a somebody?

Ayako's and Shigeo's real father's wife . . . was she a somebody? She cared enough about Mr. Itoga to keep Mrs. Itoga as her maid even after Ayako was born and she knew it was her husband's child. Then she cared enough about Mrs. Itoga to make it possible for Mrs. Itoga to keep her own children, even though she—Mrs. Scott—loved and wanted to keep the two children. She was indeed a somebody, and even today, almost sixteen years later, she was respected by people who didn't even know her.

Being a somebody . . . why, one didn't need to be rich or a white man. One needed to care about others.

I want to be a somebody some day, Sachie told herself. I want to think of and care about others, not only about myself. I wanted to gossip about Ayako and Shigeo, and I was thinking only about myself, how I would be listened to and questioned and made the center of attention. I wasn't even thinking about Ayako and Shigeo . . . I wasn't caring about them, when I like them so much.

Grow up, Sachie, grow up, she told herself as she fell asleep.

Early the next morning, Muraki-san came up the hill. Somehow he had found out the medicine man was at the Himeno home.

Poor Muraki-san, everyone called him. Poor Mr. Muraki had been looking for a wife for many years. In the beginning, he had asked for a single girl, but then he had said, "A widow will do. A widow knows what marriage is all about." But even widows did not want to work on a homestead, day after day, with sun-dried, dirt-hardened hands.

Once, long ago, poor Muraki-san had paid for the passage of a picture bride. He had gone to Honolulu, sailing from the small wharf in Konohina, to the Immigration Compound in a place called Kakaako, to meet the girl whose picture he had gazed at for over six months. This was the length of time a couple had to be married in proxy before a husband in Hawaii could send for his wife in Japan.

Poor Mr. Muraki had felt guilty, for he had sent a friend's photograph to Japan, and the girl would be looking for the man in that photograph.

When they had called his name and her name, how proud, how happy he had been to be paired with her. She was as beautiful as her picture or maybe even more so. The girl had looked at him with surprise, but did not say anything.

A preacher had married her to Muraki-san. Fifty other couples were also married that afternoon. An official noted the marriages in a book and then Muraki was free to take his bride to Kakela, to the homestead on the slopes of Mt. Mauna Kea.

Back home, Mr. Muraki would not let his wife work in the fields because she was so beautiful and she had such soft, white skin. Instead, he sent her to Fraserville to learn sewing so that she could become a dressmaker, which she said she wanted to be. That was fine, except that a tall, handsome, educated salesman from Hilo induced her to run away with him. Poor Mr. Muraki said he would forgive her and asked her to return. All would be forgotten. But she refused. Because she threatened to kill herself if he insisted, and under the Hawaiian law he had a right to insist, and because he loved her, he let her go. However, he did not divorce her, either the Hawaiian marriage performed by the preacher when she had reached Hawaii, or the proxy Japan marriage which was a Shinto ceremony followed by a recording of the alliance in the Muraki family record kept at the village temple.

A year later he was sorry he hadn't insisted upon her return, either to him or to Japan, because he heard the salesman used her for prostitution. One week she was even sent to Fraserville, where everyone knew she was Muraki's wife. Poor Muraki-san couldn't or wouldn't believe it, and insisted on finding out for himself. He hid behind a panax hedge and saw men entering and leaving. He thought of going into the house and helping her escape, if it were indeed his wife, but he waited until she would be alone.

Then it was too late, for the salesman came to pick her up. She walked out laughing and talking, almost as if she were leaving a party. He even heard her say it had been a good day, a profitable day.

Shaking and crying with shame at himself for defiling the Muraki name, he returned home. Early the next day, Sunday, he asked Sachie's father to write a letter for him, to be sent to the village office back in Japan. He was divorcing his wife, and her name was to be stricken from the Muraki records. Immediately and forever!

When poor Mr. Muraki entered the Himeno kitchen and saw a new medicine man, he looked disappointed. "I wonder if Tanaka-san left a message for me," he murmured. "My name is Muraki."

"Yes, he did," the medicine man reassured him. "He said he heard of two women in Kona, and he asked me to investigate them for you when I get there. So next time I come I should have good news for you."

"When is that?"

"Why, July . . . isn't that the usual time?"

"Yes, but . . . July is so far away . . . six months away . . ." Slowly poor Mr. Muraki walked down the hill.

Ochini no kusuriyasan! Ochini no kusuriyasan!
What? Had six months gone by already?

It was after supper that night, after old medicines had been paid for and new medicines ordered, that the medicine man pulled out two photographs. "Look," he said.

"A girl! You got a girl for Muraki-san!" Sachie's mother said joyfully. She took the two pictures from the medicine man and studied them carefully. "This one, is she part Hawaiian?"

"No, she's Japanese. But she was married to a Hawaiian fisherman for ten years. He drowned two years ago. She has three childen and wants to marry someone who will be good to the children. That is her greatest concern—the children. She's disappointed in the men in Kona, who want a good time and would even marry her if she gave the children to her mother to raise. She tried working, but the childen are still so young. They need a mother at home."

Her mother studied the other picture. "Now, what's wrong with this girl? She's so beautiful and she's still not married?"

"You're right," the medicine man answered. "This is Keiko-chan. She's blind."

"She is so beautiful, yet so sad . . ."

"Yes. It's quite a sad story they told me. When she was ten, she had the measles, and somehow she became blind. Her parents left their home and all their money to their oldest son because he promised to take care of Keiko as long as he was alive. And he did . . . till now. But he lost his wife and then remarried, last year. His present wife grumbles about having the girl in the home . . . about inconvenience, about extra expenses. So now the oldest son has asked Keiko to live elsewhere . . . get married if she can . . . so he won't have to listen to his new wife's complaints. He asked to see if we could find someone she could marry."

"Terrible . . . terrible . . . of that new wife to grumble. The same thing is going to happen to her someday. If she has a son, that son's wife will complain about her mother-in-law."

"Well, Keiko-chan's brother had problems finding a husband for his sister. The men liked her beauty, but in the long run, what would they do with a blind wife? So the brother asked that I look around on this island or some other for a man who wouldn't mind this handicap. Maybe a man with some handicap himself. He asked only that the man be a good man, who would consider her future too."

"Muraki-san is a good man."

As if by magic, at Muraki-san's name, Blackie barked, and Sachie's father said, "Ah, Muraki-san has a sixth sense."

"Muraki-san, such good news," Sachie's mother called out. "The medicine man brought two pictures, two prospects."

36

Mr. Muraki took the pictures slowly, but his hands trembled. He gazed first at one, then at the other and back to the first one again. Finally he asked, "What's wrong with her?"

"She's blind."

"And the other?"

"She's a widow with three childen."

Muraki-san studied the pictures again. "Ah, to have children in the house! It would be heaven. I would love them as my own, and they are young enough to accept me, I think, if I love them enough. But the woman, she looks foreign, harsh, angry."

"That's because she's been mistreated so much during the past two years. So many hardships. So many disappointments, I understand."

"And this one . . . do you think she wouldn't mind having a homely husband like me? Such a beautiful girl?"

"She's blind. She can't even see you," Sachie said.

"Sachie! What a thing to say," her father glared at her, while her mother pinched her arm. "Which woman would you want to live with and to share your life with, Muraki-san?"

"I could love either. But if there's a choice, I would choose this one. I don't want you to think it's because she's so beautiful. It's just that her eyes . . . you say she's blind . . . but it seems to me she can see more than the ordinary person, the way her eyes are so gentle and soft. What did you say her name was?"

"Keiko. Keiko Ohama. She can cook quite well, and even wash clothes and clean the house, as soon as she gets used to a place and the rooms are uncluttered."

"Keiko-chan . . . what a beautiful name, . . . almost like a song. Keiko-chan."

The very next day, although it wasn't even Sunday, when personal requests were usually made, Muraki-san came to ask Sachie's father to write a letter for him.

"Please, Himeno-san, I would like to have you write a letter to Keiko-chan. Please don't polish it up or take things out you think shouldn't be said yet."

"Of course, Muraki-san."

"Say, 'Dear Keiko-chan . . .' I call her Keiko-chan already . . . 'Dear Keiko-chan, today I saw your picture and I don't think I've seen a more beautiful person. I am not talking about physical beauty. It is the beauty I see in your eyes, your face, your expression. They say you are blind, that you cannot see. I do not think so. I think you see the suffering in people, the loneliness that man must sometimes bear, the pain we must undergo, together with the happiness. I think you can see the good in people just from their voices. You can recognize those who sincerely love you.

'I am not handsome or young, but my heart is good. And I need someone to share my life with.

'I am not supposed to be writing to you. By tradition, I am supposed to wait until we meet formally, introduced by a go-between. But I cannot wait. I want to tell you how good God is to me, to maybe bring me together with someone like you, to even know that there is someone like you. We are two people who need one another.

'If you marry me, I shall try to make you happy. I have some money saved, fifty acres of rich black soil where everything grows. I have wonderful neighbors who are part of my family in that we share with one another the good and the bad. They are part of my family, in that they love me. I know they will love you too and help us in whatever way they can.

'It is hard to reach the heart of another person through a letter. Someone is writing this for me, and someone must read this for you. But I hope you will understand all I am trying to say. Be sure that if you come to Kakela, everyone will love you. I hope you come and that we make each other happy.' "

Sachie said, after he had gone, "It would serve some people right, if Muraki-san got such a beautiful wife. They've been feeling sorry for him for so long."

But Sachie's father said, "And why shouldn't he get a beautiful wife? He's such a beautiful man himself."

"No woman would be loved more . . ." her mother added.

It would be hard to wait till the answer came. But, happily, they would not have to wait for six months.

* 4 *

Just Wait and See

"My mother said us guys richer than you guys," Martin said. Tommy didn't answer; instead he backed his make-believe racer about five feet, shifted gears, and roared across the schoolyard to the swings near the kindergarten buildings. Parking it skillfully in a space very few drivers could have wedged into, he got out and walked to one of the swings, where Dickie was pushing Harry, the school bully.

"Hey, Dickie, you like one?" Tommy asked, as he brought out an almost empty pack of Lifesavers.

"Thanks, eh." The lame boy's face lit up with gratitude.

"Why you gotta push Harry? He bigger than you . . . why he no push you."

"Sh-h-h," Dickie said apprehensively. "He hit you if you no push. I gotta."

Harry started up, but sat down again on the swing when he saw Tommy slip the last Lifesaver into his own mouth. "Hurry up and push," he yelled at Dickie, glaring at Tommy. Martin, who had followed Tommy across the yard, said, "We get one whole box of Hershey Kisses at our house. Sometime my mother buy gum by carton and then I chew one pack one time."

Tommy ignored him. He circled his car, and kicked a rear tire. Yep, there was enough air, all right. He got in, adjusted his racer's goggles, and drove off at jet speed, leaving a funnel of thick white smoke spiraling toward the sky. His stiff black hair, ruffled by the wind, stuck out like porcupine quills, and his eyes glinted like the tired but crafty eyes of a hunted animal. He circled the yard twice, then, anticipating the first bell, parked his racer in the shade of a banyan tree. Darn those mynah birds, he thought, as he ran his fingers over the shiny fenders of his just-polished car. The first bell rang.

The strains of The Star Spangled Banner and the sight of the flag rising up smoothly into the blue sky always moved him deeply. He saw the JPOs marching proudly into the schoolyard. Once it had hurt him that he, a sixth grader, had been rejected as a JPO. They said he was too small and skinny and nervous. As a fifth grader, he had been so sure that next year he would be able to blow the police whistle and help the little children across the street. But now he didn't care. JPO was kid stuff. Someday he would be a hero, and the JPO captain and adviser would be sorry they hadn't picked him. They'd be sorry . . . everyone would be sorry . . . only Dickie would be able to say, "Tommy used to be my friend."

"Br-r-ring." The second bell signaled the march for the homerooms. Tommy began climbing the stairs when suddenly he spied the thief who had stolen the million dollars from the bank. The thousand-dollar reward glimmered in his mind, and he wondered what he should say to the thronging reporters. Quickly he drew his six-shooter, but then he saw the innocent people who surrounded the thief, and he knew he couldn't afford to hurt them accidentally. He had to depend on his strong steellike muscles to overpower the huge, hulking thief. He dodged the people on the stairs and burst into the room breathlessly, trying not to lose sight of the crafty thief.

"Tommy, how many times have I told you not to run up those stairs," Miss Lohr remonstrated. "Look. You're all hot and sticky from early in the morning." Tommy didn't mind Miss Lohr's scoldings, because Miss Lohr was wonderful. She understood everybody. She often gave lunch money to him and to the others who forgot theirs, only the others paid theirs back. He hesitated. He had found a gorgeous caterpillar, a green and purple one. Its back was like a brand-new recapped tire, with spiky edges. Should he or shouldn't he give it to her now? But as his hand went timidly to his bag, Martin shoved him away from the desk and volunteered, "He went bang me coming up the stairs, and he went push Janet, and she went almost fall."

What a liar that darn Martin was! Tommy sat down, arranged the three telephones on his desk, and prepared for the business of the day. The phones all rang at the same time, insistently. Which should he answer first? Miss Lohr settled the question.

"Let's all sing the first three stanzas of America the Beautiful, children," she said. Everyone rose, and the screeches of "Oh beautiful for spacious skies, for amber waves of grain," echoed through the room. Tommy strode purposefully across the fruited plain.

"But General, you can't go. Why, what would we do without you?" protested the majors and colonels. They wrung their hands in agony and fright, for they couldn't afford to lose such a leader. But General Thomas Doi, first Japanese ever to become a general in the U.S. Army, was firm.

"If I'm the only one who can do the job, I must do it, even if it means giving up my life. I'm sure that . . ."

"Tommy, do sit down," Miss Lohr sighed patiently. Tommy sat down amid titters from the girls and an exaggerated laugh from Martin. "Today we are going to begin by talking about our earth as a sphere. Who knows what a sphere is?"

Several hands went up, but Tommy didn't bother raising his. He knew the answer, and he knew Miss Lohr knew he knew, for how many times had he heard Miss Lohr say to the other teachers, when she didn't know he was around, "Tommy's the most brilliant of my students. Too brilliant, I sometimes feel, for he seems to be a misfit. You wouldn't suspect it, listening to him talk, especially in his pidgin English, but he can write beautiful compositions . . . things way beyond my other sixth graders. Too bad he can't seem to either grow or pick up weight. I wonder what his home life is like." Miss Lohr was continuing, her right hand spinning a world globe absently. "We shouldn't just say the earth is a sphere. We should prove it, and by several means if possible. Well, one way was by sailing around the earth, as was done by Magellan . . ."

Tommy stared into the distance. The blue water hurt his eyes, and all he saw was water, water everywhere. There was food for only one day more, and the drinking water was going, too, even though he had secretly poured his own portions back into the barrel for the past three days. He shivered, for it was growing dark, and the cold night air stung his bones. His overcoat lined with the skin of the lion he had shot in Africa helped, but his hands were stiff. He shook them vigorously, to start the blood circulating. He didn't dare go to his cabin below, for his men were inefficient, and besides, there was talk of mutiny among the cowards of his crew. He would have to reach land . . . he must reach land . . . within two days or . . . what was that? He blinked his unbelieving yet hopeful eyes. Was it? . . . it was, and Commodore Doi jumped up in elation as he cried hoarsely, "Land! Land! A light! At last, a light!"

Loud laughter brought Tommy back into the drab, brown schoolroom. Resentfully, he looked at his classmates, his stupid classmates who seemed to think it funny if he were left out of their games. Worse, at class games, when Miss Lohr was around, the side that got him groaned, and the other side jeered. He knew he couldn't run very fast, or hit or catch a ball very well, but he wasn't that bad. When he wasn't nervous, he could catch a ball with one hand. The other sixth graders exaggerated it to make him feel bad, but heck! He could outspell any of them, and as for books, he had read more than ten or twelve of them combined, and adult books, too. Sometimes he wondered whether he wasn't smarter than Miss Lohr, for even she made mistakes in spelling, such as writing "beginning" with only one *n*. He was smart. They might as well admit that, and they did, for there they were, thousands and thousands of people who had come to honor him. He heard a senator whisper to a governor beside him, "Did you know that Sir Doi has written fifteen books already? This last one of his is a bestseller—sold three million copies. I understand his father received the Nobel Prize. Sir Doi may follow in his footsteps."

"Is that right?" the governor was replying, as Sir Doi stood on the platform, acknowledging the applause that greeted his presence. "I hear his mother is a beautiful actress—a lovely woman! He must be as proud of his parents as they are of him. Undoubtedly a very rare family . . ."

"Br-r-rin g." Recess already? Tommy hated recesses. But then he remembered. He had his racer downstairs. If they played football, he would ride around in his racer at a hundred miles an hour, to make sure no one cheated.

"Hey, no hang around me," he told Martin, who was following him with a puzzled look as Tommy shifted his gears from reverse to low to high. But Martin answered, "This free country. You no can hit me anyway. I bigger than you. Try hit me, see what happen."

Tommy was almost tempted to hit him, win or lose, when he remembered the caterpillar. Skillfully, he maneuvered his way up the stairs and to his seat. How come his bag was on the floor? And someone had stepped on it. It had been on his seat when he had left the room; now there was a dusty footprint on the peeling black leatherette. Opening the bag, he saw that the prized caterpillar had been squashed to a greenish stringy mass in the carefully blown-up paper sack. The injustice of the act smote him so intensely that for a few moments he stood staring blankly.

The sixth graders would have loved the caterpillar, especially since it seemed to have "eyes" both at its front and back. Tommy never really knew which was the front and which the back, until it started to crawl.

Unfair! Unfair! This ugly caterpillar had not had a chance to become a beautiful butterfly—maybe a Viceroy, a Monarch, or even a King Kamehameha, found only in the Hawaiian Islands. Now the caterpillar would never be admired, as it flitted from wild flower to wild flower, from climbing roses to scarlet *lehua* to fragrant orange blossoms. It could never experience freedom, after having dried its fragile wings—after emerging from the thick unlovable skin of a caterpillar. It could not enjoy a free ride as it drifted gracefully in a caressing breeze. It had lost its opportunity to become what it was supposed to become because a classmate had wanted to hurt Tommy, not an innocent caterpillar. Unknowingly, someone had destroyed one of God's gifts to Man, a gift that added beauty to the world without harming it.

Tommy drew in a dry, anguished sob, but he did not cry. Craftily, he wiped off the tell-tale footprint, replaced the bag on the seat, and sneaked back downstairs. He would act innocent, and whoever had done it would think that Miss Lohr had picked the bag up. That ought to spoil his fun! Damn son-of-a-bitch! His stepfather's swear words came to him, but they could not ease the hard knot of anger in his heart.

The day passed slowly. Several times he was in the midst of a sumptuous dinner given in his honor for his deeds as an outstanding Boy Scout. But always the infamy of the caterpillar cut into his thoughts, so that he could never quite get to the eating. First he was cold, and then he perspired, but always it was with frustration that he could not get immediate revenge.

At two o'clock it started raining. In the beginning it was only a drizzle, but then the drops began getting bigger and bigger, until soon the drops that splattered on the windowpanes were as large as half-dollars. At two-thirty, when the last bell rang, the rain was coming down in a downpour that folded the school building in its grey blanket. The children lingered in the room, on the stairs, and on the front porch. Tommy started down the stairs, and saw that the thief was still clinging to his million dollars. Tommy didn't rush this time. The thief might get suspicious. He always kept ahead of the crowd of people, for maybe he sensed that Chief of Detectives Doi was after him. Tommy had just reached the front porch with its milling crowd when he stopped, stunned! For there, just inside the hedge of the front schoolyard, stood his mother!

She stood alone, for the other mothers had not braved the rain to bring their children raincoats. Tommy saw his mother under a huge black umbrella and, under her arm, a neatly folded raincoat. From this distance, and in the rain, he could hardly see her overworked hands, much too large for her wrists or arms. Neither could he see the dirty cracks in her heels as she sloshed around in her rubber slippers. But he could see her faded dress with its uneven hemline, and the straggling gray hair which could never be kept neat. He saw her turning her umbrella this way and that, peering first at this group of boys and then that. Seeing her arms made him recall this morning with bitterness. His stepfather had hurled his cup of coffee at her because she had remonstrated against his tearing a page out of Tommy's book. She had wiped the coffee patiently but Tommy had been so infuriated then that it was all he could do to keep from getting something from the kitchen and hitting his stepfather with it. He had been grateful to and protective of his thin clumsy mother then, but here, here in the schoolyard, among his stupid classmates, he was ashamed of her. He thought of dashing out through the back entrance, when Martin called out loudly, "Eh, Tommy, there your madda." Everyone turned to look, and his mother smiled at them benignly, exposing her mouth without two upper front teeth. Mortified, Tommy ran to her, for she began coming to the porch. The cold raindrops splashing on his face mingled with his tears of shame and mortification and rolled into his faded patched shirt as he made his way homeward.

Then he remembered why he was walking home today. "Tommy, darling, would you mind walking home from school? It's the chauffeur's day off, and I have to attend a meeting, so I won't be able to pick you up," his mother had said, as she had poured more coffee for Dad from a silver coffeepot. Her long flowing gown had shimmered in the morning sunlight, and she had looked like the "Madonna" in his history book. Dad had patted him on the shoulder before he left for work, for Dad was not the mushy type and did not kiss him except on special occasions. How lucky he was, not having a stepfather who continually called him names. His Dad didn't slap his mother every time he got drunk or lost his job, and best of all, his Dad loved him, Tommy, more than anyone else in the whole world. Their house was not an unpainted shack with missing windowpanes or big cracks. His mother didn't have to take in washing and ironing, so her hands were not thick and calloused. How lucky he was, he thought again. And it was so much fun walking home. Sometimes he got bored, riding in the big black limousine, with the chauffeur so stiff and straight in the front seat.

As he climbed the steep hill to his home, he glanced back. Farther down the street, he saw Martin, walking under a huge black umbrella with a thin woman in rubber slippers. There goes Martin with his mother, to their home in the slums. Dead End Alley, they lived in, and servicemen were not allowed there. Poor Martin! Tommy opened the front door to his home, and immediately went to his room with a library book, but somehow he couldn't read. He was on his skis, skimming down a dangerous mountain to save a dear friend who had been trapped by an avalanche, when he heard an umbrella thump into its place on the porch, and the front door close. He was inching his way down the cliff, one precarious step, then another, when someone entered the room, carrying a cup of hot chocolate.

"Here, drink this. I no like you catch cold," his mother said. "Why you no hide your books when Papa stay home? You know Papa get mad with you because you dream too much. Why you no shine shoes or sell newspaper after school?"

Tommy kept his eyes closed. Perhaps if he pretended to be asleep, she would go away.

"No act like you sleeping. Your eyelashes moving." She sat on the cot and took his bony hands in hers. "Tommy, if you like, Mama and you can run away from Papa, you know. Papa not bad all the time, only when he drunk or no more money and he stay worry, but I sorry for you. Your papa—your real papa—was a good papa. Too bad you no can remember him."

Your papa? My papa? Tommy had had a Dad. Tommy's Dad had been rich and kind and had loved him. Tommy's Dad had taken him fishing and to games and . . . he opened his eyes stealthily. His mother was staring at a crack in the wall. Her dull brown eyes reflected misery and hopelessness; her half-open lips were a picture of dejection. But as he watched, her lips curved softly. Her eyes began twinkling impishly, and it seemed as if she had grown ten years younger. He watched, astonished. What was going on in her mind? Suddenly he felt a warmth, a protective feeling growing within him for her. He pulled his hand free from hers and clasped one of her hands in his. He intended giving her comfort of some kind, but instead he found himself crying. Crying because he had never been a JPO, helping other children across the street, a protector of sorts, someone the younger children looked up to. Crying because he was always the last to be picked when the class played football or other games; crying because someone had disliked him enough to stamp on his lunch bag. At the thought of the squashed caterpillar, he hardened, and the tears stopped flowing. The core of anger had grown larger and larger, taking the place of his daydreaming, which he knew now would never be enough.

"Mama, thank you for bringing me the raincoat. You the only mother who brought raincoat. You kind, you so kind.

"Mama, I going grow up big and strong. And smart! And Mama, I going make you proud of me. I going make you a beautiful butterfly —you not going to be caterpillar all your life. You wait, Mama. You wait and see . . . just wait and see . . ."

* 5 *

Second Son

That Sunday was warm, for a May. In the garden, the azaleas and gladiolas were in bloom—white, pink, salmon, and lavender—as they did almost all year round in Hawaii. The pansies stared with innocent faces, while the fuschias gently swung their miniature magenta lanterns. The asters made a tender bed of green and white. There was a heavy, sleepy fragrance in the air.

On the verandah that overlooked the Pacific Ocean, Pushi the cat stretched lazily. She measured Blackie, the dog, for a moment, then sheathed her claws into soft vulnerable paws and went back to sleep. Blackie, too, flicked an ear and closed his eyes.

Under the avocado tree in the front yard, the chickens snoozed in utter abandon, head under wing, defenseless. The eucalyptus trees bordering the west boundary languished in lazy contentment. Euphoria covered the land and everything within sight.

Sachie's father sat reading a worn magazine while her mother sewed a patch on one knee of her brother Haruo's trousers. Both Haruo and Toki had gone to gather *opihi* at Keawe, the rocky wave-washed cliffs below Fraserville, and Sachie had just returned from Sunday's Japanese school.

A car drove up the hill, stirring the dust and rattling the stones. The chickens scattered. Blackie bounded down the steps. Pushi retreated into the kitchen.

It was Itoga-san, in his work clothes. He ran to the porch, then stood there breathless, speechless, motionless.

"Come in, come in, Itoga-san," Sachie's father invited, hurrying down the steps to greet him, while her mother put the basket of sewing away. Itoga-san stood there, his mouth open. Finally her father said, "Is something wrong? Is someone in your family ill?"

"No . . . no . . ." Itoga-san said, dropping his head.

"Then what is it? Tell us, tell us quickly. We'll do anything to help . . ."

Still Itoga-san stood there. The tears began running down his cheeks, but no sound came from his lips.

"Mother, some tea for Itoga-san. Hurry!"

At that, Itoga-san came to life. "No. No tea, please. It is . . . it is . . . Haruo-san. Something has happened to your son . . ."

"Haruo? Our Haruo? An accident? Is he hurt? Is he hurt badly? Itoga-san, quickly, tell us what you know."

"No, no, he wasn't hurt badly . . ."

"Thank God! Thank Heaven . . ."

"It was the ocean. A big wave came and he . . . the wave took him. He was on the cliff with Toki, who was able to escape, but Haruo . . . they just found the body . . ."

"The body! The body? Then that means . . ." For the first time her mother spoke. "The body . . . Haruo . . ." Slowly she made her way to the Buddhist altar in the living room. She lighted a candle and incense and stared at the figure of the goddess Kwannon.

"Kwannon . . . you are the goddess of mercy . . . I pray to you every morning and every night. Why do you punish me like this?" She found Haruo's workshoes, still caked with mud, and cradled them in her arms.

"First Yoshio, my first born, and now Haruo . . . what did I do wrong in this life? Or in another life?" She wept. Never before had she raised her voice in anguished weeping. Always before, she had gone into the fields and dug the ground until she was exhausted, and her anger or hurt was diminished.

On the verandah, Sachie's father sat down again without a word to Itoga-san. His eyes stared at the land before him, at the Pacific Ocean that lay between him and his beloved Japan, at the fruit trees planted for his sons and his sons' sons.

"Was it worth it?" he asked himself. "For this land, for this freedom and plenty that we have, was it worth coming to Hawaii? I made mother come, leaving her child in Japan. I killed Yoshio, my eldest, for if I had not sent for him, he would still be alive. Day after day, mother has had to work in the fields, without relatives to visit, without a temple to pray in, without a new *kimono* these past thirty years. And all because of me . . . because I was too proud to live with my elder brother and eat his rice, which I had helped raise and which was therefore as much mine as his."

He stared at the ocean, but the tears would not come, for if they came, they would be for himself, and not for his beloved son Haruo . . . Haruo who had towered over them, Haruo who was so gentle, Haruo who had been saving every penny so that he could go to Honolulu and enter college some day. Haruo! Why Haruo, when he was so full of life? Why not me, when I have lived over seventy years and when I would willingly have given my life in exchange for Haruo's?

It was good that the Japanese families in Kakela became one extended family when misfortune fell. Sachie's father and mother were useless in making decisions. They would greet each new person who came to offer condolences, remember something about Haruo, and become numb all over again. So the Kakela family took over, the Kakela family which consisted of all of the Japanese families there.

Beginning that night and early the next day, the menfolk came to make paper flowers, lanterns, and other decorations for the grave. A Mr. Shimoda made a wooden marker, then began carving a small tablet which would carry Haruo's posthumous name . . . the name he would be known by in Heaven. The marker would be placed on the grave; the tablet would be placed in the altar.

The womenfolk cooked. Many brought vegetables from their own farms with which to feed the crowd that came. Others went into the Himeno fields to gather beans, carrots, cabbage, cucumbers. At a funeral, there was strict *shojin:* no meat, fish, poultry or even eggs could be used. Their Buddhist religion had taught them that.

Itoga-san and Togo-san, being the closest neighbors, sat on the verandah and collected donations that friends and relatives brought. The contributions were noted in a book. Then, when a friend or neighbor died, the Himeno family would be guided by the money received today, and they would donate accordingly to that family. This was the way it had been done for generations, and this was a guide for future generations.

Sachie sat in the living room with her parents. Her knees hurt, sitting on them for hours at a time. She was ashamed of herself, for wishing they had chairs to sit on. Here was her brother, in a coffin, and she was thinking of the pins and needles in her own knees. She wept because she was so selfish, thinking only of her own comfort and not of Haruo. How heartless she was. She wept even more when people patted her, because she felt so guilty. Haruo, forgive me, she asked.

During the service, the priest read the sutra, beginning with the words that were so familiar to Sachie. She remembered the many nights Haruo had sat next to her, chanting the same words. Their evening prayers had always brought them close, no matter how angry they had been with each other during the day. And now Haruo, who had seemed to cement them together in a special way, was gone.

After the burial at Fraserville the next day, close friends came back to the house to help in putting things away and in keeping the Himenos company. They all prayed again, and as they raised their voices in unison in the *kimyo muryo jinnyorai*, while the eucalyptus trees comforted each other softly, Sachie thought, "How lucky we are to have such a family of families. These people are not even relatives, yet they take a few days off to come and help and to comfort us. Do Americans have this custom too, or is it only the Japanese? How fortunate we are in being Japanese!"

At 3 A.M. that morning, Sachie woke with a start, although the house was quiet. There was only the steady ticking of the clock on the table. Something, however, had awakened her.

Then she realized Haruo was gone. She had listened to her brothers Toki and Haruo plan his going away to Honolulu to college for four years so many times, his leaving had been no surprise. Haruo had really left for Honolulu to enter the university there, she had said to herself earlier. He would return in four years, to help the Japanese in Kakela and Fraserville diversify their crops and form a cooperative. So he wasn't really dead.

But at 3 A.M., she knew he was gone forever. His big dream had been crumpled and tossed into the ocean, to float for a while and finally to merge with the blue-green water. Haruo's life was only a dream. It had been a good dream, a long dream, but still it had been only a dream. The memory of it would fade away. Big, friendly, thoughtful, energetic Haruo would fade away from their lives. It would be as if he had never existed, just as Yoshio, the first son who had died in Japan, had never existed for Sachie until a few months ago. Was this what life was, only a string of dreams, of memories?

Sachie's tears flowed silently into her pillow. How could Haruo be a dream, he of all people who had affected so many others? She wept, and her nose clogged with her tears. But rather than blow her nose and wake her family, she breathed through her mouth.

Suddenly, someone, somewhere in the house, blew his nose. He, too, must have had a clogged nose from weeping. It must have been that weeping, silent though it had been, that had awakened her. Her father . . . surely it was her father . . . for he would never cry in front of people.

Haruo was gone, but her father was alive and needed someone to love. Love me, Sachie commanded her father in the dark silence, love me, because I love you too. Love me and let me take the place of Haruo. I cannot tell you I love you in words, in English or in Japanese, because we Japanese never seem to say such things. We only show our love in our actions. Haruo, tell Mother and Father I love them. Tell them right now.

In her intensity to send this message, Sachie forgot to breathe through her mouth and blew her nose. The silence in the house was intensified. The tick-tock of the small clock boomeranged against the walls of the room to tell them that time was passing by, that life is only a dream for everyone anyway.

On the seventh day after the funeral, the priest recited: *"Sore ningen no fusho naru so wo, tsura tsura kanzuru ni oyoso hakanaki mono wa, konoyo no shi-chiu-ju maboroshi no gotoku naru ichigo nari . . ."*

"Life is only a dream," the priest interpreted. "From beginning to end, it is unreal, fleeting. A lifetime passes soon. You go or I go first, and we don't know when that will be. This is fate . . . all we know is that we cannot know the future. That is why we pray for God's love with our prayer *Namu amida butsu* daily, so that God can be our strength in our weakness and in our uncertainty."

Why, that is what I thought, Sachie realized. Life is really only a dream. Some religious person, many years or centuries ago, had written so.

On the fifteenth day after Haruo had drowned, her mother said, "Come, we must all go and pay our respects to the ocean that took your brother."

"No," Toki protested. "I don't want to go to that place again." His brother had been taken and he had been spared. Why?

But Sachie's mother cut some flowers from the garden, gathered incense and candles, and took Haruo's harmonica from a special drawer. Toki finally drove Sachie and his mother down the dusty, curving road that led to the cliffs of Keawe. Her father refused to go.

Keawe was a beautiful spot, and Sachie could not imagine how anyone could die at such a magnificent natural garden. Sheer precipitous cliffs rose up and up, almost touching the sky in their limitless height. One cliff wall showed every shade of green, from the olive yellow of the *kukui* trees to the velvety black in the crags where the light could not penetrate. The other wall was golden. The low afternoon sun cast a warm glow over all the trees, and the tiny leaves of the trees twinkled like so many golden bells, as if to sing out their guiltlessness of any wrongdoing. The ocean before them was green and turquoise blue and purple; it was calm and innocent. But on the cliffs to one side, where the *opihi* and other shellfish clung, the waves dashed in frustration, churning the water angrily in a million evanescent bubbles, bubbles that were real, that existed for one brief moment, then vanished forever. Sometimes the lower portions of the cliffs lay bare, as the waves receded, and the teeming sea life clinging to the walls lay exposed, vulnerable but treacherous, as if they shared a secret pact with the wild waves.

It was to these cliffs, to this foaming portion of the sea, that they had come to pay homage.

"Here, take this," her mother said, throwing Haruo's prized harmonica into the water. "And don't take anyone's life again. Be satisfied with Haruo. For we loved him so much, and you have taken him away from us."

When they returned home, her father was playing his flute. It was the piece called "The Dawn Wanderer:"

> And he wandered, in the fresh and spotless dawn
> To the rustling of the bamboo and the swishing of the pine,
> And the path was narrow, though the sky was wide and endless
> And he wandered, searching, searching, for his destiny he must
>   find.

Sachie could almost hear the bamboo, as they rustled their dry, prickly narrow leaves. The dark green pine would swish like silk tassels of the sugarcane on a dry, windy day. The dew on the grass lining the path would cling to the wanderer, but the traveler, intent on the road before him, would be unaware of the wetness or of the beauty around him. He must go on. He had a destiny. But what was his destiny? Was this destiny more important than the path with its diamond-studded grass glittering in the early morning sunshine? Was an eternity more important than a moment?

When Sachie left for the kitchen, she saw her father on the verandah put his head in his hands, but a few minutes later, he took his flute and played a tune they all loved and had listened to at least once a week during their lifetime.

* 6 *

Graduation

It was the day before graduation. Sachie picked two hundred white carnations and sat down to string them into a triple carnation lei. The lei would be for her neighbor Ayako, for her brother Haruo had planted the carnations for her, who would have married Haruo had he lived.

After stringing the carnation lei, Sachie started on a pansy lei. The pansy lei was for Miss Case, the English teacher, who had been at Fraserville for three years and was now being transferred to a Honolulu school. Being assigned to Honolulu was almost every teacher's goal.

Sachie smiled, thinking of her many tussles with Miss Case in the one year she had had her for English.

Once, Miss Case had wanted her to sit next to Chiyo, who had lice crawling over her black hair. Sachie refused to move.

"I'm going to have to send you to the principal," Miss Case warned. The threat did no good. Better to be sent to the principal than to have lice and have one's hair doused with kerosene.

"Why don't you do as I say," Miss Case pleaded. Sachie couldn't say, "Chiyo has lice," even though everyone in the classroom, including Chiyo herself, knew it. By putting it into words before others, she would make Chiyo lose face. So Sachie was silent and sent to the principal's office with a sealed note.

The principal, who knew Sachie as his daughter's best friend but also as the girl who had spilled smelly cod liver oil on his best suit one day, read the note.

"Now, what's the matter?" he asked. "Miss Case says you don't want to share a seat with another girl. Don't you know we don't have enough seats, and we all have to share where we can?"

"Not just another girl. Chiyo!" Sachie explained.

"What's wrong with Chiyo?"

"She has lice. Her mother should use this special kind of comb my mother used when I caught lice from her before. The teeth of the comb are so close together, it draws out the lice. Then her mother has to wash Chiyo's head with kerosene. But she has to wash more than once because the nits hatch, and then there's lice all over again . . ."

The principal turned pink. "Did you tell Miss Case why you didn't want to sit next to her?"

"In front of everybody? You think I want to make Chiyo feel shame?"

The principal wrote a note and gave it to Sachie to give to Miss Case. Since it wasn't in an envelope or sealed, it couldn't be very private. Sachie sneaked a quick look. All it said was, "Lice. Health Room."

Another confrontation Sachie had had with Miss Case was when she was sitting next to Rose. Rose had a habit of reading her words out loud when she concentrated. "Participle . . . participle . . . participle?"

One day, Miss Case was correcting papers and said, "I'll give you free time today to review the chapter for tomorrow's test. You have lots to do, so I don't want to hear any whispering or talking. Is that clear?"

Concentration . . . Rose studied every sentence, every word, mouthing her words. Sachie read her chapter, then looked at Rose in amazement. How could Rose know what was in the chapter if she read words instead of the ideas in the combination of words and sentences?

Just then Miss Case raised her head and noticed Sachie's head turned toward Rose. "Sachie, I thought I just said I didn't want any talking."

"I wasn't talking, Miss Case."

"Now you're lying, which is even worse."

"Ask Rose. Ask her if I was talking to her."

Rose turned red and lowered her head. To Miss Case, that was proof Sachie had been talking to her.

"Sachie, I told you I don't like people who lie. Will you please stand outside the door until you can learn courtesy for other members in the class."

The injustice, the unfairness of Miss Case not even checking with Rose, and Rose not answering when Sachie asked her, was too much. Sachie grabbed her books, and instead of standing outside the door, walked to the cafeteria. There, the cafeteria manager, thinking her one of the student helpers, scolded, "Where's your cap? Put your cap on. Don't you know you're always to have a cap on when working in the cafeteria?"

Sachie found a cap in a corner, put it on, washed her hands and then helped to spread butter on the bread. It wasn't real butter . . . it was peanut butter which had had milk added to it to make it thinner and to stretch it.

At first she buttered the bread angrily, but soon she began enjoying it. She had finished this job and was being assigned another, when a girl came dashing in.

"There you are! Sachie, Miss Case is looking all over for you. She even went to all the bathrooms and to the principal's office."

Sachie remembered. She was supposed to be standing outside the English classroom door.

"I didn't talk, and Miss Case said I did. She accused me of lying in front of everybody. She made me lose face."

"We know. Miss Case found that out. She heard the talking even after you left so she watched us. She found it was Rose reading aloud. She said she would give Rose extra help in reading, and she apologized for accusing you and began looking for you."

So after the fall came the pride. Miss Case was extra nice to her for weeks after that.

As Sachie sat stringing the pansies for Miss Case's lei, she thought of all the times Miss Case had shown interest in the homestead children. She was different from the other teachers. Miss Roe, for instance, never got angry with anyone and was never unfair, but she didn't care what happened to the students after school. Mr. Gobel was snobbish, and tried to associate with the white people in the big houses on the hill, although they never invited him to their parties. Mr. Rhodes was nice, but he acted as if the homestead children were beggars, just because their canvas shoes had holes at the toes or they had no shoes at all. But Miss Case, she was different.

"Go through high school, and then to college if you can," she encouraged. "With your intelligence, your alertness, it would be a shame to spend all your life working as laborers—planting cane, pulling weeds, cutting the cane—when you can become doctors, lawyers, even representatives and senators in Congress if Hawaii ever becomes a state. I have faith in you to become leaders of your community and to contribute to it."

"We have the ambition, but we don't have the money."

"Don't be afraid to work while going to school. You can work in cafeterias. In Honolulu, you can work as maids and yardmen. That way, you get free room and board. You can work at the pineapple cannery during summers for spending money, for tuition. You can apply for scholarships."

To those who had a hard time in learning school work she said, "But college isn't the only important place where you learn. You can learn while you work. The important thing is that you be happy, doing the work for which you're best suited. If you're going to be a chicken farmer, be a good one. If you want to be a mechanic, be reliable, for people's lives depend on you. That's such an important job."

As Sachie strung the lei, she thought, "Funny, about this time last year, I used to think most white people didn't respect the Japanese or Portuguese from the homestead and looked down on us. But look at Miss Case, who cares so much about each of us."

A carnation lei and a pansy lei made with hundreds of flowers and hundreds of memories . . . that was June. June was the time friends and teachers parted, the end of a school year. June was the time those who graduated began making something of themselves. June, and not January, was the month when a new life, a new year, really began.

* 7 *

The Sacrifice

In June, Ayako Itoga would graduate from high school. It was the first time a Japanese girl from Kakela would do that. Always before, the girls had been docile, and listened to their parents' requests to drop out of school to work or to get married.

But Ayako had been different. She had refused to quit school or to get married. She refused to attend a *miai*, a meeting where a boy and a girl and their parents with the "go-between" could talk and eat with each other without any commitment expected. Ayako would slip off and take long walks in the woods. She ignored the angry words heaped on her during the evening.

In many Kakela homes, they discussed Ayako almost as if she were their own daughter.

"See? It was a mistake, allowing her to finish high school. Now it's college she wants."

At the Itoga home, Mrs. Itoga said to Ayako, for the hundredth time, "It's out of the question."

"I have to go. Whether you allow me or not. Brother says he'll work twice as hard while I'm away."

"You know we don't have any money. How can we afford to send you through college?"

"All I need is enough to go to Honolulu. Cost by steerage is not much. My teacher, Miss Case, found a place for me to live. A professor, his wife, and four children need someone to help with the dishes, the laundry, and to stay with the children at night."

"A maid! Mother, she intends to be a maid!"

"Miss Case worked as a maid while going through college. Lots of girls do that, she said, because it means they can have free housing and breakfast and dinner. They are even allowed to take sandwiches for lunch," Ayako explained.

"Mother, tell her what happens to maids!"

"What happens to maids?" Mrs. Itoga demanded of her husband. "Times are different, Father. My reason why she shouldn't go to college is, who on this island . . . what Japanese boy . . . would marry a college graduate? How many Japanese male college graduates can we find on this island? And if she marries in Honolulu, we will hardly get to see her or the grandchildren."

"A maid! Impossible!" her father still insisted.

"Times are different, Father," Mrs. Itoga said. "Also, Honolulu is different from the plantations."

"Different? There is no difference. There is no difference in men living in Honolulu and on the plantations twenty years ago or today. Get a pretty single girl in the house—and you know Ayako is beautiful—and sooner or later they act the same."

"This is a professor, Father . . ."

"A professor is still a man, Ayako."

"Are you saying all men are alike? Including you?"

"I'm saying that when there is an opportunity . . ."

"Our case was different, Father, and you know it," Mrs. Itoga whispered, as if in deep pain.

"Oh, so now it's my fault, what happened to us . . ."

"I didn't say it was your fault. Or my fault, either. I said our case was different. And I did things by choice."

"But it's my fault because I forced you, in a way, to make the choice you made?"

"No, I was the one making the choice," Mrs. Itoga said. "Ayako, you are old enough to know the whole story of why you have blue eyes instead of black or brown. Let me explain how it happened."

"You don't need to, Mother."

"I know. But I want to, Ayako. You know your father and I were

62

married in Japan. Your father came first because we weren't sure we would want to live in Hawaii. I was to come if he liked the islands and when he had saved enough for my passage money. To save money, your father didn't eat properly or buy warm clothes. After working all day on the plantation, he would go into the mountains to get firewood just so he could make extra money. Sundays, he washed and ironed for other men who sat and gambled. And when I finally came, we found he had TB. He had TB, this hardworking man, and the men who played and gambled, they had no money and no wives, but at least they had no TB.

"The plantation bosses wanted to send us back to Japan, but they didn't want to pay our way because your father hadn't worked his full three years. We didn't have any money to buy tickets to go home on our own. The Japanese men in the camp were kind, but they didn't want your father in their camp because they were afraid they would catch TB too. I wasn't strong enough to work on the plantation and I wouldn't be able to earn enough to support your father and myself.

"Then one day the plantation boss came to tell us that we had to leave the camp. He was afraid the other men would also catch TB. We didn't know where to go, but we had to start packing what little we had. Then, two days later, the plantation boss came back to tell us that he had described the situation to his wife, and she had said she needed a maid. Not just any maid. Me! There was an empty cottage behind their house that we could live in. Ayako, you don't know, you can't possibly know, how grateful, how happy we were.

"The missus, she was so good to us. She taught me to speak some English. She called me her little doll.

"But one day, when the missus had been away for a week visiting Honolulu, the boss called me to his room. I thought I had done something wrong. But when I found out what he wanted, I said 'No!' I couldn't do that. I came back to the cottage to tell father we would have to leave, after all. I saw him sleeping. He had some color in his cheeks, and he was gaining weight. He was getting rest in a quiet place, medicine from the hospital, and good food, for the missus always made me make more than they needed and told me to take the left-overs home. If we left that home, where could we go? What would happen to your father?

"I stayed, and when you were born a year later, I wanted to kill myself because you had such sparkling blue eyes and I knew you would have a difficult life."

"But I wanted to kill myself too," Mr. Itoga interrupted. "Each day, I would say, today I am going to kill myself. But when I saw your mother bringing me soup or eggs from the kitchen, I knew I couldn't kill myself. For then, your mother's sacrfice would be for nothing. I couldn't kill myself, but do you know how it felt? A man is supposed to support and protect his wife, yet here I was making my wife support and protect me."

He poured himself a drink of *sake*. "No, instead of killing myself, I lived each day ashamed for you."

"Is that why you drink *sake*?" Ayako asked. "Because you're ashamed of me? Well, I'm not ashamed of myself. I don't care that I'm half-white. I study harder. I work harder. That's why I was offered a university scholarship. That's why I'm going to be valedictorian at the graduation exercises next week. You may be ashamed of me, but I'm not ashamed of myself."

"Ayako, Ayako," her father broke in, "don't misunderstand. Ashamed OF you? Never! Ashamed FOR you. There's a difference. I'm ashamed and sad I'm not your real father. I'm ashamed I had to depend on your mother for survival, after all the plans I had made, all the dreams I had dreamed. But I'm not ashamed of you, Ayako. No, I'm so proud of you. When I heard you were going to speak to the whole community at graduation, when I heard you were selected above all others, I was so proud. No, Ayako, I'm ashamed FOR you, but not OF you."

"I don't see why you have to be ashamed, father. You say you are ashamed because mother had to support you when you were ill. What's wrong with that? Wouldn't you have supported mother if she had been unable to cook or do the laundry or work in the fields?"

"Of course. But that's a man's job, to support his wife."

"A man's job? According to tradition, yes. But what if the man is unable to do so for one reason or another? Isn't love and helping one another when one is ill stronger than any tradition? That's what mother did, in whatever way she could."

"Ayako, Ayako, what are you saying? Father, don't listen to her," Ayako's mother protested.

"No, mother, let me finish. Father is riddled with guilt, and he's been carrying this guilt too long. Father, how many nights have you made mother get up from her bed because you had this guilt and you had to drink *yake-sake?* Moher had worked all day in the fields and she needed her rest, but your guilt was stronger than your consideration for her. You made her get up from a warm bed to comfort you. Are you a strong man, making her do that?"

"Ayako, stop!"

"No, let me finish. Father has had this guilt complex for too long. He thinks people are laughing at him, when people accepted the fact that Shigeo and I are *hapa haole* long, long ago. By this time they could care less. So why is Father still carrying guilt and shame and pampering himself? Why is he living in the past? Father, take this guilt burden off your back and my back and Shigeo's back and make your next eighteen years more productive ones. Appreciate what mother did for you in the only way she could.

"And, father, please tell me you want me to go to college, since I am going anyway. Tell me to carry on with your plans, your dreams. Let's make your early dreams a family affair."

* 8 *

The Fighter

Few foreigners walked the streets in Japan in 1875. The entry of U.S. Commodore Matthew Perry's threatening Black Ships into Japan waters with a requested trade treaty, first on July 8, 1853 and then in February 1854, was only two decades in the past. The Japanese looked with sidelong glances in curiosity and distaste at any "hairy" foreigner. Marriage between the two races, or anything more than a business relationship, was unthinkable.

But Joseph Higgenbosom, a tall handsome English silk merchant, met a young Japanese girl in Yokohama, and from this union was born a child who grew up proud, handsome, defiant, and aggressive. Fred Kinzaburo Makino, who took his mother's name, was born in August 1877. When he was five, his father died.

It is said that Fred had a happy, carefree youth, and was a lover of teahouses where he learned to sing and dance with the best *geishas*. His mother decided to send him to Hawaii, where his brother Jo had a small store in isolated Naalehu, Hawaii, believing Fred would have to settle down in such a primitive, foreign environment.

Twenty-two when he arrived in Hawaii in April 1899, Fred tried working at his brother's store, but that job, as well as clerking positions at Kona Sugar Refinery and at Honokaa Plantation, was too boring to suit Fred. Little did he realize that an office position was a coveted one not readily available to the Japanese in 1900. Fred Makino was intelligent, charming, and Caucasian enough to be able to win what were considered such highly desirable office jobs.

Instead of "appreciating" his so-called "good fortune and opportunities," twenty-four-year-old Fred moved to Honolulu in 1901 and opened his own Makino Drug Store at Nuuanu and Hotel Streets.

He too caught sight of a slim, doe-eyed young girl, daughter of a storekeeper called Okamura, who had emigrated to Hawaii in 1885 on the *City of Tokio*. On April 7, 1903, when she was less than fifteen, Fred Makino married Michiye Okamura.

Two years later, in May 1905, when she was only sixteen and helping to care for pigs on the Makino farm in Manoa, a suburb of Honolulu, she heard that over 1500 Japanese plantation workers out of over 2225 field and mill hands went on strike at Lahaina's Pioneer Mill. The strike began when a *luna*, a foreman, beat a worker, accidentally blinding him in one eye. The angered coworkers demanded the discharge of that *luna* and four others, as well as improvement of their living quarters and sanitation facilities. To assist the planters, the then governor sent special police and National Guard members, armed with field artillery, on the S.S. *Kinau* from Honolulu to Maui. By the time they reached Lahaina, the town had quieted down. The Japanese Consul General and other community leaders spoke to the workers. Two of the foremen were replaced, and minor grievances settled. Young as she was, Michiye Makino became aware that her husband was angered by the stories in the papers, and a new light flickered in his eyes. Every action of his, even feeding the pigs, seemed charged with energy.

Only four months later, 1500 of the more-or-less same workers struck, asking for a 15-cent raise in daily wages and an eight-hour work day instead of the ten hours they worked. They lost.

In 1906, 1000 plantation workers struck in a small plantation called Onomea; they asked for a $1 daily wage, or $26 a month. Again the workers lost. Nothing could dent the strength of the plantation owners and managers who banded together with one another through the Hawaii Sugar Planters' Association. The Japanese workers had no such organized strength at this time.

Managers of plantations had been warned by officials of the Hawaii Sugar Planters' Association, however, that Japanese and

Chinese laborers could not be treated as they had been from 1885 to 1900:

> In times past we got too much in the habit of treating the Japanese and Chinese as if they were more animals than men. We cannot do this now, and it is not likely that the Japanese will stand being so treated when they themselves are an extremely polite race. So, while you must not give way to loafers for a moment, it would be well to be firm in a more kindly manner than was the custom ten years ago.

The *Hawaiian Gazette* of May 6 also warned in an editorial that

> It will be a good thing hereafter for plantation *luna*s to remember that they are not dealing with laborers of a servile and inferior race but with the sturdy and self-respecting subjects of a power with means to assert itself in the world as an equal. . . . The class of men used as *luna*s is not credited with coolness of judgment and kindness of disposition.

Japan's war with gigantic China and China's defeat (1894–1895) and Japan's war with equally gigantic Russia and Russia's defeat in 1905, had bolstered the pride of the Japanese plantation laborers, and they refused to be treated like slaves, since they were nationals of what they considered a mighty country: Japan.

By 1909, the Japanese laborers' fight was not against brutalities inflicted on individuals or of contract violations, but for equal pay for equal work. It was pointed out that the Portuguese earned $19.53 a month, the Chinese $17.61, and the Japanese only $15.58. But, the plantation owners countered, the Japanese had a lower standard of living, so needed less money than the other races. To the Japanese who had to work in the dark in vegetable gardens to supplement their food, this statement was adding "insult to injury."

Makino, who had a pig farm as did many other Manoa Valley residents, realized that an organization was needed even for pig raisers. A Pig Raisers' Association was organized, of which he was elected president. He realized that in numbers there would be strength. Aware that with a sugar plantation strike, there would have to be cooperation not only among the plantations, but with the community as well, he and twenty others discussed problems of coordination, financing, and morale. There had been about 1125 labor disturbances where the laborers pitted their strength against management, not only among the Japanese but among the Chinese, Korean, Portuguese, and Puerto Rican workers. Rarely had labor been successful, for plantation managers realized that to accede to demands would mean other strikes would inevitably follow.

When 7000 plantation workers struck on May 9, 1909, Makino and some other leaders were psychologically and organizationally ready. The group coordinated an Association for Higher Wages. Its chief demand was to ask for an end to racial discrimination in wages and to request the same pay scale for the same work done. It was a reasonable request and the Japanese community was in sympathy and promised support.

A mass meeting regarding the strike was held at a theater, and the building overflowed with 1700 workers. The leaders, including Fred K. Makino, editor to the *Nippu Jiji* Yasutaro Soga, attorney Motoyuki Negoro, reporter Tokichi Tasaka, and Matsutaro Yamashiro proposed and asked for $22.50 a month, knowing full well the plantations would not grant the request.

The community came together as if someone had waved a magic wand, even though two small Japanese papers were promanagement.

Some of the plantation managers wanted to settle the strike by granting the higher wages which they felt the workers deserved, but other managers prevented them from settling because "it would seem we are being controlled by foreigners."

The strike separated relatives and friends, as some family members joined in the strike, and others did not. Sometimes a family purposely remained at work so that some financial assistance would be available to others.

Workers notified their employers that they would be striking, and when told they would have to vacate their homes with all their belongings, they replied they would clean the house and premises before leaving.

There were trains from Waipahu and Ewa to Honolulu, but none from Kahuku to Honolulu. Mothers walked the long fifty-mile distance, carrying a baby on the back and holding on to toddlers. When it grew dark, the families strung along the roadside to rest and sleep. Men must have wondered if they could find a job in Honolulu, women whether they would have a roof over their heads, and if the children could continue going to school.

The next morning, they walked the rest of the way, climbing Nuuanu Pali's steep, treacherous road into town. And in the town, there was uncertainty too. How long could the residents of Honolulu feed the thousands upon thousands that came limping in, weighted down with clothes, babies, and pots and pans?

The managerial task of feeding and housing the evicted strikers in different areas of the city—Palama, Kakaako, Moiliili—was immense. Food had to be collected and meals cooked and carted to centers three times a day. Some families cooked enough for ten; association kitchens prepared food for hundreds. Thousands had to be fed, day after day, month after month, from early May to early August.

Negotiations continued on some plantations, and some strikers were able to return home after less than a month. Other plantations refused further negotiation; in a way, these plantations lost, for the strikers began work in town as mechanics, carpenters, painters, plumbers, and in the offices of Japanese business firms. When the strike finally ended, these experienced plantation employees decided to remain in Honolulu.

Four leaders—Makino, Soga, Negoro and Tasaka—were tried at the end of the strike and imprisoned for their part in the strike. The charge: attempting to "impoverish the plantations." The jailed men were released from prison less than four months later under a special pardon by Acting Governor Mott-Smith. In the days that followed, the names of Makino, Negoro, Soga, and Tasaka became household words in the Japanese community.

Much of his earlier life, Makino had been a playboy of sorts. While in prison he had the opportunity to associate with Editor Soga, Reporter Tasaka and Attorney Negoro, who were deeply concerned with the welfare of Japanese immigrants in Hawaii. Makino's world-view changed. He was henceforth to play a new role in Hawaii, a role that required fearlessness, persistence, aggressiveness, and a canniness designed to outwit the opponent.

So when, on June 10, 1909, a High Sheriff broke into the Makino Drug Store to confiscate, then dynamite open his safe to take what were supposedly "records" or confidential documents of the 1909 strike, Makino boldly sued the plantation owners for the damage done and for their unconstitutional act. His friends warned him that he could not possibly win a law suit in the Territory of Hawaii; the plantation owners and high government officials were too friendly with each other and too powerful as a combined unit. But Makino would not withdraw his suit. After a long drawn-out battle, the two sides agreed to an informal settlement.

It was after the strike that Makino decided to enter the newspaper business. In a December 7, 1912 issue he wrote:

> This paper, to be published daily in the Japanese language, will endeavor to the utmost of its ability, to further the interests of the Japanese residents of the Territory of Hawaii. This paper is not subsidized by the planters, nor, on the other hand, is it the organ of any Japanese society or institution . . . it is free . . . and will give an unbiased opinion as to any question that may hereafter arise.

And so the iron-jawed, quick-thinking *hapa haole*, having tasted challenge and having matched wits with top plantation lawyers, had his appetite whetted. As his wife later said, "My husband was a fighter. He believed in fighting for the rights of the underprivileged. He would go to bat for the underdog." He was the Don Quixote of Spanish literature, fighting for the human rights of the Japanese immigrants.

There was yet another strike, the strike of 1920, to test his fighting spirit. The strike of 1920 involved 2000 Filipino and 4039 Japanese workers. Over 2643 wives and 3856 children were evicted from their homes. Housing, food, and sanitation facilities again posed problems of magnitude.

Actually, Makino did not support the 1920 strike as he believed the plantation workers were making satisfactory wages. Union bosses had begun to organize the laborers, and were supposedly spending "thousands of dollars on entertainment and pleasure," using union funds. Also, the organization of labor unions was such that strike strategies were falling into the hands of plantation managers within an hour after they had been agreed upon. Makino stated that something "smelled." After all Makino's efforts in the earlier strike, union headquarters now called Makino an enemy and said he was plotting to destroy the unity of the workers.

The strike ended in failure. Both strikers and plantations lost financially. But wages increased in a few months, and water supply and housing conditions improved. Over a thousand families remained in the city as they had obtained jobs or had become small shopkeepers during the strike.

Makino's service to education is also well documented. He skillfully battled the Territory of Hawaii despite lack of funds, political ostracism, economic pressure, oppression, and scorn by plantation and government officials, and the fright of many Japanese *issei* and *nisei* afraid to support Makino openly.

During the early pre-World War I years, the Japanese celebrated the Emperor's birthday on November 3, no matter on what day of the week it fell. Japanese children were excused by their parents from attending English school, and families congregated at the Japanese school to witness certain rites carried on by the teacher or principal, such as the reading of the Imperial Edict and the singing of the Japanese national anthem, *"Kimigayo."*

This was an occasion of solemnity with the undraping of the Emperor's framed photograph and the reading of the edict to the photograph, instead of to the parents and children assembled. No child dared to whisper during these few minutes. Whether such awe could be equated to patriotism is subject to question, but this loss of a public school teaching day brought the charge that Japanese schools were actively teaching patriotism to Japan.

A Federal Survey Commission in 1920, in the wake of antiforeign language schools reaction following World War I, recommended that the Territory of Hawaii abolish outright all such schools, suggesting that when the demand for learning a foreign language arose, the Department of Public Instruction could offer classes after regular school hours, taught by teachers employed by the department. Teachers would have to pass standardized English examinations and be conversant with American history and government, including democratic ideals and institutions.

The Special Session in 1920 passed Act 30 which provided that "no one could conduct or teach in a foreign language school without a permit from the Department of Public Instruction." The Territory also passed several laws in 1923 and again in 1925 that were against Japanese language schools. One that angered the Japanese community was the act that required a head tax of $1 per student while attending a foreign language school, with civil and penal penalties for nonpayment of this tax Also, the Territory provided for elimination of grades kindergarten through grade two the first year, then grades three and four in the following years. This would have eliminated Japanese schools altogether.

To keep Japanese schools open, it was first necessary to have a Japanese school begin litigation against the Territory, a terrifying move for the usually meek and unaggressive Japanese. There was intense hatred and disdain directed at Fred Makino, who was heading the drive to keep the foreign schools open. The fear of the Territory's revenge against principals and teachers, and even against parents and children who participated in the litigation, plus the possibility of economic bankruptcy and future harrassment prevented any one principal from stepping forward to initiate the litigation. Makino stood alone and waited.

Then, on December 28, 1922, Futoshi Ohama, principal of Palama Japanese Language School, courageously stepped forward to sign the necessary papers!

The reason for his taking the first and necessary step had a story behind it. When Futoshi Ohama had first arrived in Honolulu on the

S.S. *Shunyo Maru* on June 12, 1917, he and two other Japanese school teachers were denied entry and were detained at the Immigration Center. New laws regarding immigration had been passed less than two weeks before, in which the Territory and the Immigration Office stated that entry was limited to two categories only: (1) wives, children and picture brides whose husbands or parents were already in Hawaii, and (2) businessmen. Teachers were classified as new immigrants, and therefore were not allowed entry.

In a court trial held in Honolulu, a petition for a temporary landing privilege was defeated. But an appeal to the Ninth Court of Appeals in San Francisco brought forth the decision that specially trained language school teachers were not ordinary immigrants. The territorial government and the Immigration Office then appealed to the Supreme Court, which ruled that entry was permissible. The battle lasted a long, full three years from 1921 to 1924. Futoshi Ohama never forgot this prolonged fight on his behalf by Fred Makino.

Because of his *on* or obligation to Editor Makino, Principal Futoshi Ohama stepped forward to begin litigation against the Territory to prevent the government from closing Japanese schools. Soon other schools and principals joined Ohama, and in the end 88 of 146 Japanese schools joined as co-petitioners in the school test case. They were fighting for the constitutional right of a group of people to provide education in their parents' language and culture for their children.

The fight to keep the schools open had been a long, uphill, seven-year battle, especially for Editor Makino who against great odds and economic pressure fought almost single-handedly in his quest for justice. Sometimes he was unable to purchase newsprint for his newspaper, either on credit or for cash. Often his newspaper employees were paid late. Yet they persevered to keep the *Hawaii Hochi* going so it could tell its readers what was happening in San Francisco, then in Washington, D.C., on the test case.

The decision which stated that no one has the right to interfere with the right of parents to educate their children was made public on February 21, 1927. The law was to be applied equitably to all residents of the United States regardless of race, which meant that in twenty-one other states, foreign language instruction such as German, Italian, and Spanish could continue. Various state regulations and restrictions were declared unconstitutional and therefore illegal. Hawaii, although only a territory, had, under an immigrant, Makino, paved the way for all states to continue foreign language instruction for their children!

There was a giant celebration on March 29, 1927, with 5000 people present, but it was a sobering moment for Editor Fred Makino, for his purse was empty, his cupboard was bare, his employees were either underpaid or unpaid, and his wife was pale and weary from seven intense years during which she saw her husband sleep for only a few hours each night.

With victory came donations, but it had been a long, grueling, lonely seven years, with hatred, malice, and ill will from government officials radiating about him, and the need to be constantly alert, making him watch every word said or printed. But the value of these Japanese language schools was recognized with great awareness during World War II, when young men with knowledge of the Japanese language were able to make vital contributions to their country as censors, interpreters, and especially in the intelligence field. It is said that the knowledge of the Japanese language by these and other young men cut short World War II by two years, thus saving the lives of thousands of fellow Americans.

The love Makino had for his fellowmen demanded many sacrifices; he experienced poverty, ostracism, and the threat of physical harm. But he put the welfare of the people above his own, as he struggled for equality and justice at a time when the Japanese immigrant worker was "low man on the totem pole" in Hawaii.

* 9 *

Communion

It was quiet, deathly quiet, and that was strange, for Morio Tamura's life had always been full of sounds. There had been the crickets and cicadas on the Tamura farm in Japan, and the rustle of canefields and harsh commands of foremen on the sugar plantation in Hawaii. Here, in Honolulu, the sheathed thunder of cars, buses, and trucks from below his locked and heavily draped bedroom window merged wih his everyday life. Sounds and noises were taken for granted, like the air around him, yet now there was this depthless, monotonous silence.

Was it time to get up? He had to be at the delicatessen by 4 A.M. if he wanted the coffee and doughnuts to be ready by 5 A.M. A few faithful customers always came early for breakfast. What time was it anyway? He tried to open his eyes but couldn't. He then tried to reach for the clock by his pillow and again he couldn't. He didn't even hear the tick-tock tick-tock that put him to sleep every night. Am I dreaming, he wondered. Then he fell into a motionless sleep once again.

The next time he awoke, he noticed not only the silence but the chill in the air. It was . . . it was . . . was there such a thing as antiseptic chilly? As if one were being preserved in a tub full of alcohol?

The tub reminded him of his iron vat with bubbling oil in which he made his doughnuts. How many more cases of oil did he have in the storeroom? And flour . . . should he order another forty bags? The newspapers talked about a shipping strike in a few weeks. But if the strike wasn't called, then he would be stuck with the flour and somehow the mice always got to the flour sacks. The health inspectors didn't like that.

Time . . . time to get up . . . what time was it? Surely it must be almost 4 A.M. Why was it so quiet and cold? Where was Mama? Where was the alarm clock? I must be really exhausted, he thought, and fell asleep once more.

Two nurses entered the room in the morning, one with some towels and the other with a tray of thermometers. The first one said, "Mr. Tamura . . . Mr. Tamura . . . I'm going to wipe your face, okay?" The second slipped a thermometer under Morio's tongue.

The first nurse asked, "How many days is it since he's been in a coma? Forty? Fifty?"

"More like ninety, " the second nurse answered, examining the chart at the foot of the bed. "Ninety-seven today, to be exact."

"You think he'll ever come out of it?"

"Hard to tell. He's a tiny man . . . only five feet tall and weighed 110 pounds when he was brought in. He's 76 pounds now. But he looks like a scrapper, a fighter. The other day I was giving him an alcohol rub and it seemed like he tensed his right arm. First time I felt that. So he could be coming out of it."

"Sad . . . being pistol-whipped for a few dollars. Honolulu was never like this. I can remember when we used to leave our windows and doors unlocked all the time . . . even at night."

"I know. Now I don't feel safe even in my own garage. And I lock myself in the car when I drive."

"Kind of a shame, isn't it, someone in a coma lying in this private air-conditioned room. He can't even appreciate it, yet he has to pay for it."

"The police wanted him here. Anyone coming here has to pass through two stations."

"Must cost the family a fortune. I heard a rumor Admissions suggested the family take him to a Japanese hospital, when they found out he didn't have any health insurance."

"You can't blame the hospital. But we took him and kept him, didn't we?" She picked up her tray. "Hey there, Mr. Tamura, brave man, you in your secret world, have a nice day, huh!" She left, followed by the other nurse.

Morio Tamura, in his secret world, faintly heard Mama calling him. Or was it his mother in Japan? No, it was Mama. "The paper cranes," he thought. "The paper cranes Mama's making for my sixty-first birthday party. What fool originally thought of making 1000 paper cranes for a sixty-first birthday party, and what fools made this into a tradition? Fools with time, that's for sure."

I wish we had had a daughter, he mused. A daughter-in-law is okay, but a daughter is different. Now I understand why Mama used to say that if we're going to have only one child, she would have preferred a girl to a boy. Even if the boy can carry on the family name.

He thought of Tom, his son, and Evelyn, his daughter-in-law. They were good kids, kind and considerate, but somehow not as close to them as a daughter would have been. His friend Shoda had a married daughter and always on Sunday afternoons this daughter brought some food over for her parents . . . "so you don't have to cook tonight" . . . she said. Then she cleaned the kitchen, scrubbed the bathroom, and sometimes the inside of the refrigerator while her husband talked to her father. How lucky the Shodas were!

It must be time to get up and go to the shop. Surely it must be close to 4 A.M. What would the workmen say if the shop wasn't open by 5? They depended on him for coffee, doughnuts, and biscuits. Where else would these truck drivers and construction workers have their large but cheap breakfasts? I must get up. But I can't open my eyes. Am I drugged? How could I be? Am I dreaming? Wake up, Morio Tamura. You don't have time to be sleeping. But he fell into another deep, unconscious sleep.

A few days later, Mrs. Tamura sat folding her paper cranes in the hospital room, as usual.

"*Otoo-san*," she whispered, "*Otoo-san*, papa, can you hear me? Wake up! Try! You've got to come out of this coma. You can't die without saying goodbye to us. At least to me. Wake up! Look, I already made 800 cranes. Only 200 more to go, and remember your birthday is only a few months away. You've got to be well by then. I sewed your red kimono for the party, and we have the guest list. So wake up, *Otoo-san*, for how can we have your birthday party without you?"

Mrs. Tamura sighed. After three months she was exhausted with anger and worry. What would happen to them now? Should she sell the shop? Maybe the new owner would hire her. After all she was still strong at fifty-seven, and she knew all the customers. Would she have to depend on charity in her old age when she had worked steadily for thirty-five years, minus six months before and six months after Tom was born? Thirty-four years of hard work in America, the land of the free and the home of the brave, Tom used to sing. The land of justice, of plenty, of love. And a land where someone wanted to kill her husband for a few dollars!

"What kind of country did you bring me to," she asked. "I gave up a country where I had relatives and I could understand the language. In that country I don't think anyone ever pistol-whipped or attacked another person from the back, even in feudal days of long ago. The Japanese fought man-to-man, from the front, with warning. Why did we come to these islands? What happiness have we had, working from four in the morning to nine at night, every day of the week?"

She pounded her husband's body in anger, heedless of different tubes attached to his body. "They say this country has justice, but there's no justice. The police didn't even bother looking for the boy. They said they had no clues. They just wrote something down on a piece of paper, that's all. They just accepted it . . . it wasn't anything unusual to them to have someone almost killed by another. When I try to talk to them they just move away. *Otoo-san*, how can you die now? You didn't have your party. You didn't see the 1000-crane tree. What about the trip to Japan? You said we would all go to Japan on your sixty-fifth birthday . . . when you retire! Lies . . . all lies! You aren't even trying to come out of your coma. It's easier lying in this air-conditioned room than working in a hot delicatessen and standing on your feet all day. You don't care about us . . . you're taking the easy way out."

"What? What?" her husband mumbled. "Four o'clock already? Time to get up, Mama?"

Mama . . . Mrs. Tamura . . . was so shocked she forgot to ring the bell to call the nurse. Instead, she ran to the door and yelled, "Nurse! Nurse! Come quickly. My husband just talked to me!"

Two nurses came running. "Mr. Tamura . . . Mr. Tamura . . . do you hear us? Can you understand? You're in a hospital and we are taking good care of you. You have nothing to worry about. Your wife is sitting right here. Mr. Tamura . . . Mr. Tamura?" But Morio Tamura was back in his deep, deep sleep.

"Are you sure he spoke?" a nurse asked. "It wasn't a moan? Or a gurgle?"

"No," she answered, "he asked if it was four o'clock already."

"Four o'clock? Why four o'clock?"

"That's when he used to get up to go to work every morning."

"You're sure it wasn't wishful thinking? You didn't imagine it?"

"I'm sure. He spoke clearly." The nurses waited. But they had many other chores, Mrs. Tamura knew. So she said, "Thank you. Maybe I did dream it, after all." She picked up her bag from the floor, extracted some paper, and began folding a crane.

After the nurses left she leaned over Morio and whispered, "So! You make me look like a fool! Why did you stop talking? Listen, Papa, I know you can hear me. By the time I have my 1000 cranes, I expect you to be out of your coma. You understand?" she scolded gently.

When, several days later Morio next awoke, he felt his mother pushing him. "Morio-chan, Morio-chan, wake up. Wake up and work in the fields for a few hours. Remember, your brother is sending you to high school. You must work hard before and after school since he's making this sacrifice. Be grateful to him." '

Be grateful to his older brother? But Morio knew why his brother was sending him to high school. Ever since Morio had contracted diptheria when he was twelve, he had stopped growing. Now he was fifteen and still so small he was of little use on the farm where strong labor was needed. His brother was hoping that with more education

Morio would go to some city, get a job, and not be dependent on his older brother.

"I would be grateful if I hadn't heard my brother discussing this with my sister-in-law one night," Morio thought. "They were talking of ways to get me off the farm for good. They made me feel so unwanted. I wish I had never heard them talking about me."

So he continued sleeping although he could feel his mother pushing and pulling him . . . maybe even washing his face? Now why would his mother wash a fifteen-year-old's face? He wanted to protest, but instead he fell into his deep sleep again.

Five days later Mama said, "Well, that's the 1000th crane. Now I'll have to tie them to the tree branch Papa got from a friend. We have the invitations ready . . . "

"Mama, did you get white print on red paper or red print on white paper?" Morio asked, as if he had been in conversation with Mama all along.

Mrs. Tamura trembled and dropped the crane she had been holding. It took her a few moments to say quietly, "White print on red paper."

"Good. It'll be easy to read. Remember we had an invitation once with red print on black paper and we had to hold it a certain way to read the invitation? Poor Mama, 1000 cranes! But now you can relax a little."

"I enjoyed making them," Mama said, hoping one of the nurses would walk in on the conversation. "Somebody come . . . somebody come . . ." she prayed.

"Come to bed, mama. We have to get up early tomorrow morning, as usual. I had a long day, standing on my feet, and they feel like lead bars attached to my body. I can't even move them. You sleep early, okay?"

"Sure . . . sure . . . as soon as I put my things away."

She pressed the bell. When two nurses came in she said, "My husband spoke again. Right now. He asked about the color of print on the invitations we made for his sixty-first birthday."

The nurses looked at each other. "That's wonderful, Mrs. Tamura. That's a good sign he might come out of his coma soon. Now listen, there's nothing more you can do for your husband tonight so why don't you go home and rest? We'll take good care of him."

So they still didn't believe her. But it didn't matter. It was a matter of days or weeks before he'd come out of his coma. Papa was getting better and look what a clear mind he had. "Yes, I think I'll go home and rest," she reassured the nurses.

It was a week before Morio spoke again. "Where am I? I dreamed I was in Japan with my mother."

"You're in a hospital, Papa," she told him. "Remember someone hit you on the head with a pistol?"

Mrs. Tamura definitely saw a muscle twitch in his face. "Oh, I remember. A boy . . . a man . . . came in and bought doughnuts. One-half dozen. He paid me and as I was going back into the kitchen I felt something hit me. That's all I can remember. How much money did he take?"

"All that I left in the cash register before I went home. About $6 in dollar bills, nickels, and dimes."

"Strange . . . he looked like such a nice boy. He talked so softly. I gave him two extra doughnuts because I had only two left. He told me he just wanted six and I said the extra two were free. He said 'Thank you.' By the way, when can I leave here? I have to order some flour, in case we have a shipping strike later in the month."

"We already had a shipping strike, Papa, and it's been settled so don't worry about the strike."

"We had a strike? But it was supposed to begin June 15."

"It's September 9 today."

"September! How can that be? When it was June 2 yesterday."

"You were in a long coma, unconscious, Papa. But thank Heavens you're okay now. Listen, I'm going to call one of the nurses. They didn't believe me when I said you talked the last time. Talk to them . . . the nurses . . . so they'll know you can really talk."

When Mrs. Tamura returned with one of the nurses, Morio was

again in his deep motionless sleep. The nurse sighed in exasperation, but with sympathy. "Hang in there, Mrs. Tamura," she comforted her.

For another long ten days Morio Tamura slept, like an empty sack with tubes going into and out of him. Mama talked to him, pushed and pulled him, whispered, shouted, scolded, whimpered. Had he really talked to her? Even her son Tom wouldn't believe her, so she herself began having doubts.

"You know, Mama, when we wish and dream for something, it seems true," Tom told her. "You wanted Dad to come out of his coma and you wanted him to talk to you, so you heard him. It had to be in your mind, because how come he doesn't talk when anyone else is around?"

But the very next day he opened his eyes for the first time, although he couldn't move his head or hands. "Mama, forgive me," he said. "I lied to you. Well, I didn't exactly lie, but I didn't tell you how short I am, when I asked my brother to find me a wife in Japan."

Mrs. Tamura was surprised. He was now talking about what had taken place forty years ago, when she had come as an unseen bride. How his being short must have bothered him!

"I didn't want to tell you how short I am because I was afraid you wouldn't come to marry me. . . . The white people on the plantation used to call me 'shrimp' and the plantation boss told me to work in the kitchen because I'm so short . . . like a girl, he said."

"So what?" Mama answered. "I lied to you too. I told the go-betweens not to tell you I'm 5 feet 3 inches tall. At all my *miai* in Japan the mothers turned me down because they said I was big and clumsy. They wanted a dainty daughter-in-law, one they could show off to their friends and neighbors. But a few months later they were regretting it because the daughters-in-law didn't even want to wash the dishes and the mothers had to cook and clean the house and become servants for the dainty wives. Hah!"

"Mama, remember when we were first married? When we took snapshots I always took them on steps. I would stand one step behind you so I would look taller. How it bothered me, being shorter, yet I was happy because I had a tall wife and I wanted tall sons."

Mama waited for his next words but he closed his eyes, sighed, and went back to sleep.

The doctor and nurse came in, just a moment too late to hear Papa talk. By now Mama refrained from telling the nurse about Papa holding a conversation with her.

"How is my husband?" she asked the doctor.

"As well as can be expected," the doctor replied.

"When will he be completely out of his coma?"

"What do you mean . . . completely out of his coma?"

"Well, sometimes when he talks to me he's clear about things, but then other times he thinks I'm his mother, I think. When will he not go back to sleep again for days at a time?"

The doctor and nurse looked at each other. "We've had cases where patients have been in coma almost ten years," the doctor said. "Then we've had patients who came out of a coma perfectly normal and patients who couldn't remember anything or recognize anyone. We don't know about Mr. Tamura."

"Papa's mind is clear, and of course he recognizes my voice."

"Remember, when your husband does regain consciousness, if he ever does, he may not remember much because of the brain damage and massive hemorrhage," the doctor warned.

"But he does remember," Mrs. Tamura insisted. "He even asked about the color of print used on his sixty-first birthday invitations."

The doctor looked at his watch. "Fine . . . fine . . . let's keep waiting and hoping and praying. Miracles can and do happen. Now would you mind waiting outside for a few minutes?"

"What about this case, Doctor," the nurse whispered after Mrs. Tamura left the room.

"Damage was extensive to the brain area . . . plus the hemorrhage . . ."

"It's a wonder he's still alive, isn't it?"

"He got hit two or three times on the back of his head, at the nerve center. And he was hit by a strong young man, the way his cranium was fractured. I think the paralysis is permanent."

"Poor man. Better if he had died right away. Now maybe he'll be a burden on his wife for years and years, and they don't even have health insurance. Personally, I'd rather die than be a vegetable fed by tubes."

"Sometimes you don't have a choice. Sometimes the next of kin don't have a choice too. Unless laws are changed." They left, and Mrs. Tamura entered to find her husband sleeping peacefully.

Eight days later Morio opened his eyes and said, as if he had not been unconscious for more than a week, "Listen, Mama, will you promise me one thing? Listen carefully, now. In case I turn out to be a bedridden invalid, if I'm completely paralyzed, promise me you'll help me to die."

"No. How can I do such a thing . . ."

"Mama, please, won't you help me?"

"Even if I wanted to help you, what could I do?"

"I don't know. A healthy man can die in a car accident or drown in the ocean or fall from some tall building. But if one is bedridden and especially if he's like a vegetable, how can he die when he wants to? I don't know, Mama. That's where I have to depend on you."

"What are you talking like this for, just when you're getting well. Every day you're getting better, you know. I don't want to hear anymore. Besides, visiting hours are over, and I have to go home."

"Please, Mama?"

"No!"

"It's my only request. From my only life partner. For the sake of my life partner."

"I don't know what you're talking about." But she reached out to him. His thinness pained her. How could a man's arm really feel like a stick?

"Mama, is it daytime or nighttime?"

"Nighttime."

"Could you open the window and please turn my head so that I can see out?"

"There's nothing to see out . . . only a few stars."

"Stars? Oh, I want to see the stars . . . I never had time to see stars while I was working. Remember when Tom was in kindergarten and he had to sing 'Twinkle twinkle little star' all by himself for a Christmas play and we practiced and practiced together with him?"

"And the teacher scolded him because he sang 'Twinkoru twinkoru litoru star . . . raiki a diamondo in za skai.' "

Did he chuckle? Mama thought so, and she too smiled. But then he seemed to have fallen asleep again so she left.

Morio opened his eyes and saw the stars. As he gazed at their shiny brilliance they seemed to break into little pieces and slide earthward, together with his tears that slid down his cheek to the pillow.

The next morning the nurses called cheerfully, "Good morning, Mr. Tamura. And how are we today?" But instead of wiping his face, one of the nurses called the doctor right away.

"Too bad Mr. Tamura passed away without regaining consciousness. In a coma 136 days so he's really skin and bones," the nurse said.

"It's a wonder he lasted this long," the house doctor agreed.

"Kind of sad," the nurse said. "You know, there was such love between them, Mrs. Tamura is sure Mr. Tamura spoke to her several times. But that's physically impossible, isn't it? His throat muscles were paralyzed as much as the rest of his body, so he couldn't have talked, could he?"

"Most likely not," the doctor agreed. "But then there's a great deal we still don't know . . ."

The nurse pulled the pillowcase from the pillow. Strange . . . it was wet, as if with tears.

* 10 *

Banzai, Col. Rogers, Sir!

I t was March 9, 1942. Soft fluffy snow covered rooftops, bushes, and ground. It rested lightly on branches of trees and made little mounds on fence posts. Icicles hung from eaves. Two weeks ago there had been a blizzard and the mercury had plunged to 15 degrees below zero. But today it was a gentle, silent white world.

Into this serene peacefulness clanked and clattered a decrepit train, spouting clouds of black smoke. It expired with a giant yawn and exhausted hisses.

Officials in Camp McCoy in Wisconsin had been alerted that the Hawaii Japanese internees were coming. Undoubtedly envisioning dangerous fifth columnists who had been instrumental in the devastation of Pearl Harbor on December 7, 1941, the camp commander had thirty steel-helmeted, battle-ready soldiers at the station, bayonets poised for action.

The last car with the frail and elderly was unloaded first. Forty of the internees stumbled out. All wore heavy long GI overcoats which had been issued to them before they left Hawaii, but underneath some wore flimsy aloha shirts and lightweight trousers suitable only for Hawaiian weather.

They shivered as the cold penetrated the overcoats, and they stretched shoulders, arms, and legs to exercise the stiffness and exhaustion out of their bodies. Yet they touched the soft snow, piled high along the hedges, almost in delight, as they viewed the quiet beauty surrounding them. They looked old, dried up, mummified,

89

because they drooped with fatigue and weariness and were covered with soot, yet at the same time they looked like little children, eyes sparkling and lifting a finger of snow in wonderment and admiring its delicate beauty.

Unknown to them, the camp commander must have issued an order, for the bayoneted soldiers disappeared. By the time the last train car had been emptied, all that could be seen were many under-sized bodies in oversized overcoats lining up as usual for the next sharp command.

It was almost dark and biting cold when the first contingent of Hawaii internees reached Camp McCoy, Wisconsin, that March 9. The camp had served as Civilian Conservation Corps barracks during the Depression years in the early 1930s. There were rolling hills, pine and oak groves, and a huge military training area within its 20,000 acres. Farmhouses, barns, and silos dotted the approach to the camp.

There were about a hundred European nationals already at the camp, including Catholic priests, engineers, musicians, and profes-sors of languages. Most of the men were well-educated professionals who had been born in the "wrong" countries: Italy, Germany, and Hungary.

The exhausted Hawaii men found they could take a hot shower after the sooty, bone-tiring trip. Their four barracks had two stoves each which warmed them both physically and psychologically. Later, they found that it was a "drifter" from Oregon, an itinerant who had worked on the railroads and picked fruit on farms in many states who had attended to the boiler room and provided heat for the eight stoves. He did not know any of the Hawaii men, yet he had worked hard to make their entry into Camp McCoy comfortable. The Hawaii internees compared him to six well-dressed Japanese international businessmen from Seattle; they found the "drifter" sincere, humble, and thoughtful.

Each internee was issued three blankets, two sheets, a pillow, and a pillowcase. For the first time since being picked up on December 7, 1941, the men slept between clean sheets; they slept well, after the exhausting three-night, four-day train ride.

Soon after their arrival a new commander was assigned to the camp. He was Lt. Col. Horace Ivan Rogers, a Detroit lawyer in civilian life.

"Gentlemen," he addressed them, "I welcome you to Camp McCoy. I want you to know that we respect you, for you are not criminals. You are not being held for acts committed against our nation. We are merely detaining you, who are enemy aliens, for reasons of our own. If you have problems or concerns, please have your repesentative make an appointment with me and I shall try to be of service to you."

Rogers realized how traumatic the change in weather could be for these men coming from Hawaii, especially dressed as they were, for one day he announced that roll call at night would be at 9 P.M. inside the barracks, just before lights were to be turned off. The internees were astonished, especially since he often came into each barrack alone, leaving his two guards outside. He nodded to each man as he clicked his hand counter. At this moment, the opportunity was there for anyone to approach him with any complaint.

Because Rogers was so kind, Masao Sakamoto, the chef, asked if the internees could celebrate *Hanamatsuri* or Prince Siddharta Day on April 8. This day is to Buddhists what Christmas is to Christians. Rogers agreed, but asked that he be allowed to attend the festivities.

Rev. Hakuai Oda, an expert in the art of making artificial flowers and in floral arrangement, made cherry blossoms by dyeing toilet tissue in diluted beet juice and fashioning pink petals. He attached these to a dry oak tree branch. The result looked almost like a real cherry tree. And, like a real tree, petals occasionally fell, as if to symbolize the passing of time and the transience . . . the impermanence . . . of life.

Col. Rogers, who had donated cake and fruit for the occasion, got up and addressed them. "Gentlemen," he began. It was as if an invisible cloak of gentlemanliness had enveloped each of them, and their affection for this officer shone in their faces. If he thought they were gentlemen, they would be gentlemen. They would not, could not, let this man down.

91

The days passed. The internees seemed contented enough, as they stumbled to the diningroom in other people's footsteps. Food was plentiful, and, with volunteers in the kitchen, tasty enough. The men ate and slept, slept and ate. They obeyed passively and meekly any and all commands. They looked, in their overcoats, like bulky silk cocoons . . . without personality, without individuality.

To the perceptive physician's eyes of Dr. Kazuo Miyamoto, the men looked like zombies. "Col. Rogers," he reported, "the men are deteriorating both physically and mentally. These men were leaders in their community. They were always active. They need to be involved, even in a camp such as this."

"Any ideas?" Col. Rogers asked.

Together they discussed possible activities. As a result, Rogers brought in used gloves, balls, and bats for the young and athletic. Teams were formed and these challenged one another, working toward a camp championship. Now the younger men ignored the cold weather, and came back to the barracks eyes alert, faces ruddy, and voices ringed with laughter and triumph.

The older men liked to polish stones they found. Pebbles from the age of lava and glaciers made beautiful semiprecious jewelry. Col. Rogers had three truckloads of stones dredged from the lake bottom brought to the camp. The men eagerly sought certain pieces; in their minds they could see the result of shaping and polishing.

One night, as spring limped in after a long winter, Col. Rogers entered their barracks. It was already 10 P.M., an hour after lights had to be out. Some men were asleep. Those awake wondered what they had done wrong, or whether they were to be moved in the middle of a cold spring night to yet another camp.

"Gentlemen, have you ever seen the Northern Lights?" the Colonel asked.

"The what?"

"The Northern lights," he repeated, pointing to the stars outside.

"Yes, every night, when we were at Sand Island in Hawaii," they replied, thinking he meant stars in constellations.

"Why don't you put on your shoes and overcoat and come outside?" he suggested.

Some of the men were suspicious; perhaps they were going to be transferred again. Remembering the days when they didn't even have a handkerchief, they changed into a suit and stuffed belongings into a duffel bag before donning their overcoats, heavy socks, and shoes.

The world around them was still and frosty—a black and white picture. But as they stood, stamping because of the cold, a change came over the black sky. It shone several shades of silver, a very pale blue, pale green, and a hint of lavender and pink. It looked as if God had suddenly turned on a million volts of pastel-colored lighting for some sort of celebration.

Few of the men had ever seen an aurora borealis before. Its delicate beauty and grandeur was such that it seemed almost supernatural. Because it was unexpected, it was doubly dazzling in its majesty. They loved it and they loved Col. Rogers for inviting them to share in this phenomenon.

Days and weeks, including spring, came and went. The men still looked ragged, in their one suit of clothes, as they waited anxiously for their suitcases and for their promised $50, held up somewhere. Finally, in May, just as the warm season began, the winter clothes arrived, too late to use until the following winter. But the men felt closer to home with the arrival of their clothes, for each item had been numbered by hand by a family member. The $50 they never received.

But it didn't matter. In May, they were told they could receive up to $30 a month from home. What a great day that was! The last time Kumaji Furuya had fingered cash was when Sho Tominaga of Samoa had given twenty of them a dollar each, some months ago. He had looked longingly at all the items that could be purchased for a dollar. Again and again he had mentally selected and added his purchases. His final decision: three 20-cent airmail stamps, 13 cents soap, 10 cents toothpowder, 6 cents cup, 5 cents coughdrops, 5 cents candy, and 1 cent match.

Also in May, they received letters, some months old. Someone even received a telegram from Japan! The men were exuberant. Now they were part of civilization again! They could be in touch with their families!

A few weeks later, the men were informed they were to report to a camp farther south. Camp McCoy was to be the training grounds for the 100th Infantry, a battalion made up of Hawaii National Guard members and volunteers into the Army.

When the Camp McCoy internees left Wisconsin, they were told only that they were being moved south about 800 miles. This time it was a short twenty-four-hour ride, as compared with the exhausting four-day, three-night ride from San Francisco to Wisconsin. The men were not guarded every minute; in fact, they had to make their own sandwiches in a car adjoining the diningroom.

When it was announced that they would soon be at the train station, they looked out the window to see a plateau with groves of huge oak trees. They learned the elevation was 2000 feet above sea level, and the town close by was Tullahoma, Tennessee, close to Georgia and Alabama. These three states were not in the internees' travel vocabulary, like California and New York.

Camp Forrest, their destination, was two miles away from the train station, and large enough to accommodate 40,000 troops. As the men were taken to their quarters, they noticed that there were both black and white troops there, but they were in separate units. And now here was a yellow unit, an unarmed unit. This unit was to be surrounded by barbed wire fences, watchtowers, guards, and dogs! They were to be prisoners!

Accommodations for the internees had just been completed. The huts, built for five men each, were of knotty pine. The green wood was warped and did not fit well together. Chill air filtered in through cracks, but the men were not seriously disturbed. They knew that with hammer, nails, and scraps of lumber, such defects could easily be remedied.

The men lined up for army cots, thin mattresses, pillows, and sheets. By this time most of them could quickly set up a cot. Those who finished early helped others.

Food at Camp Forrest was good and plentiful. They could even have all the sugar they wanted. The first night, seeing there was more sugar than would be needed, some of the men ladled sugar into clean paper napkins for use in the future. But the next day they saw the sugar bowls had been refilled. Finally, reassured, they returned the "borrowed" sugar back into the sugar bowl. "We're lucky," they commented. "I understand back home sugar is rationed."

Unlike at Sand Island and Camp McCoy, lights at Camp Forrest could be on till 11 P.M. and they could sleep till 7 A.M. The men were more contented than they admitted, especially since they had self-rule, attended classes, could engage in hobbies, and receive money and letters from home. Now, just as they had collected shells and coral at Sand Island to occupy their time, they turned their attention to collecting fossils. It became a consuming desire to find a fossil and make it into a watch fob. The men seemed to lose their individualism in their desire to have what the others had—in this case, a watch fob.

This desire related to clothing too. At Wisconsin, they had all worn Army woolen trousers and Mackinow coats, originally purchased in the 1930s for Civilian Conservation Corp youth. In Tennessee the woolens were taken away and the men were issued green shirts and pants. Strangely, these clothes fit. It was as if the uniforms had been made especially for them.

Later they learned why. A shipment of these uniforms had been made especially for Philippine scouts to use in jungle warfare. But with the fall of Manila to the Japanese, the American ship had returned to the mainland United States with the uniforms still in the hold. Some bright quartermaster must have seen the size of the uniforms, realized they were too small for American soldiers, and put his memory of Japanese internees to good use by getting uniform and men together.

The uniforms were bright green when first issued, but under the

Tennessee summer sun turned to a mottled greenish tan. Soon an internee asked the supply officer for some green dye. One day this enterprising internee appeared in a bright green uniform again.

How nice he looked! He stood out from the rest of the men in their faded uniforms. The others wanted to know how he had done it. Within a few weeks almost everyone appeared in bright green again. Now the internee in the faded uniform stood out in that section of the camp.

Furuya remembered how he used to tell his wife not to copy women who wore different fashions as the styles changed—from long hemlines to shorter hemlines, from no sleeves to puff sleeves to raglan sleeves to peplum sleeves. It was "monkey see, monkey do," he told her. "Don't be a copycat. Be yourself. Wear fashions that compliment you."

And now here he was, anxious to have his uniform dyed green, just like the others. He was forgetting about ideas, commitments. What had happened to him in just a little over six months? How had he changed so? What had made a community leader and successful businessman overwhelmingly concerned about the color of his clothes? Was this what brainwashing meant? Did this happen to all incarcerated men, no matter how pleasantly incarcerated they were? He almost chose not to dye his uniform, in protest, but his desire for a fresh green shirt and trousers overcame his desire not to give in to conformity.

During the hot days that began in June, the men gathered on benches set in oak groves. These were the coolest spots available, and they spent their time reminiscing about the past and wondering about the future.

With the heat came the flies. They buzzed on the food, in the huts, under the trees, everywhere. Finally the men organized a fly brigade, since they didn't have any spray to control the insects. Armed with folded newspapers, the brigade systematically battled the flies, as if they were the enemy.

"Here, take this!" A fly lay with tiny legs moving feebly.

"Hah! Three at a time!"

"You are the enemy and you must die!"

"Whom are you killing, the American soldiers or the Japanese soldiers? Which side is the enemy?"

The swatter looked surprised. "Why . . . the enemy is the enemy. The ones we're supposed to hate."

"The Americans have us locked up in this camp, far away from home. Behind barbed wire. With machine guns pointed at us, daring us to escape. Are they the enemy?"

"How can the Americans be the enemy? My wife is an American. Some of my brothers and sisters are Americans. My friends and children are Americans. Can my children, my relatives, my friends be the enemy? Sure, we're in camps, but are we behind bars in cells like in a real prison? Are we starved? Tortured? Didn't the Americans take care of Bishop Kuchiba when he had appendicitis? I don't like being interned, but that is not saying the Americans are my enemy."

"The Japanese soldiers then? Are the Japanese military the enemy, since they force the common people to engage in war?"

"How can the Japanese be my enemy when I'm Japanese myself. I was born there. Japan must be my country since I am not allowed to become an American citizen. How can the people of my country be my enemy?"

"Who, then? You said you were killing the enemy. Who is this enemy?"

"The enemy," the man answered, swatting another batch of flies, "is someone I don't know, haven't seen, and whose face I can't imagine. He doesn't have human characteristics, such as kindness and honesty. If he's a human being, someone with parents who worry over him, grandparents who watched him grow, children who wait for him to return, and a dog that licks his hand and face, how can I hate him enough to kill him?"

"In other words, then, an enemy is not a person. It is just a word, an idea . . ."

"I suppose so. The enemy is faceless. Until our government puts the word and people together, and they become one. The 'idea' of an enemy merges with the man through propaganda in the newspapers and on radio. A man we have never seen whose background we don't know about is made to become our enemy."

"This is too complicated. Let's just kill flies. They're insects, not the enemy. And let's hope the soldiers bring back some insecticide when they go into town the next time."

With the transfer of internees by Col. Rogers from Camp McCoy to Capt. Laemmle of Camp Forrest completed, Rogers was to return to Wisconsin and to other duties. But before he left, he told Capt. Laemmle that this group of men were gentlemen and asked that they be treated as such.

On the day he was to leave, the Hawaii internees gathered in front of the dining hall. Rogers shook each man's hand, wishing him well. Then, as he said his final goodbye, the internees' voices resounded in a spontaneous cheer. "Col. Rogers, *Banzai! Banzai! Banzai!*" This was the greatest gift the men could give him, for *banzai*s were at one time restricted for the emperor. Perhaps it was the first and only time prisoners incarcerated in an enemy camp cheered and showed their esteem and respect for their jailor. *Banzai! I hope you live ten thousand years!* The men were acclaiming and honoring the spirit shown by Rogers: his fairness, his understanding, his kindness, the humaneness with which he had administered his camp.

Banzai! What did it matter that Rogers was Caucasian and they were Japanese enemy aliens? His words, his actions had not been influenced by ethnic or national considerations. He had ignored race and position during a critical period of suspicion and distrust. He was a man and he had treated them as fellowmen.

"*Banzai! Col. Rogers, Sir!*"

* 11 *

You Can Go Home Again

Yuki scrunched into a fetal position on the narrow hotel bed, her stomach twisted in a pain that left her breathless, a gnawing, lacerating pain that was not physical, not something for which one could take pills.

It had been a long, lean ten years, as she and Jeffrey had seen their life savings disappear month after month after month, even though they had worked at double jobs for the past five years. Now a decision had to be made, for their savings had been depleted. Was this what they had worked for, ever since their marriage over thirty years ago? To be middle-aged and again penniless, as they had been when they had gotten married?

After days, weeks, then months and even years of frustrating discussion, they were finally forced to return to Hawaii to take Mother home to California, although she had stubbornly refused to move each time they had asked her. But now, there was no alternative. They were unable to meet medical and nursing fees. Medicare had been exhausted long ago. It would be much cheaper for Yuki to quit her two jobs and stay home to care for her mother-in-law. They installed a fence and a gate that could be locked, for Jeffrey's older brother Wade had told them Mother would slip out for walks and forget the way home. The police had often been called to assist in searching for her. Once, she had fallen into some tall grass in a ditch, and, unable to climb out, had not been found till the next morning. Luckily, it had been a warm and dry night, and she was still asleep, although covered with mosquito bites, when found by some young boys looking for grasshoppers. Meanwhile, neighbors and friends had searched frantically for her all that night. So finally, Yuki and Jeffrey had agreed to Wade's suggestion that, against their mother's wishes, they move her to a nursing home.

What to do . . . what to do . . . but was there a choice? Yuki took a deep breath, exhaled . . . took another deep breath, exhaled. "You can exhale all your problems away," a psychologist friend had assured her. "Breathe deeply . . . hold it . . . exhale. Breathe deeply . . . hold it . . . exhale. There, don't you feel better?"

Yuki had nodded, but she knew no matter how many deep breaths she took, the problem causing the gnawing in her stomach would not go away. It had nothing to do with relaxing; it had to do with the decision they would have to make regarding Mother. Was their ultimate responsibility to an immigrant parent who had sacrificed so much for her sons? Or was it to their own daughter who would be attending college in the fall and who needed the best education possible to cope in an increasingly complicated world?

There was another alternative, according to Jeffrey. They could request assistance from the state, provided Mother was penniless. The state, after a thorough investigation, would then take over nursing home payments. There was no guarantee where Mother would be placed, or what kind of care she would receive. She might be placed in a home where no one spoke her language, and she would not be able to communicate her needs to them. It was therefore a heart-wrenching alternative that wrought anguish and shame, and a feeling that filial piety was lacking, which had been drummed into them from an early age. A Japanese family, whether in Japan or Hawaii, takes care of its own, they had been told many, many times. That is a son's responsibility. But with today's medical costs so high. . .

"If we take care of Mother at home, we might be able to send Darlene to Stanford, since she has a tuition scholarship," Yuki kept saying.

Yes, there was no alternative except to take Mother to California, even if she protested. Already they had sold her home, the home Jef-

100

frey and Wade had been born in, to pay nursing costs. Mother's savings were gone; now Jeffrey himself had nothing left in his own bank account, even though he had paid only half of the expenses of the nursing home. Wade had paid the other half.

Of course, Darlene could go to the community college, which was almost tuition free, and she could live at home. But poor brilliant Darlene . . . would she be getting the education she deserved?

Yuki covered her head with the top sheet. She wept tears of frustration, of uncertainty, and yet of relief that they would once and for all have to make a firm decision.

Across the room, Jeffrey let out a deep sigh. So he too was troubled! Even in his dreams . . . even in his dreams . . . Yuki wished the roosters would crow so they could begin another day.

Tomorrow . . . or today, since it was 3 A.M. . . . she would be revisiting the home she had been born in, over half a century ago. There, she told herself, she would be able to regain some of the security and serenity that had been hers as a child.

She dredged the memory of the house and yard, and lingered over each tree and room. Here were the three pine trees her parents had so carefully brought from Japan. They grew straight and tall, unlike the gnarled, windblown pines clinging to rocks and cliffs in Japan. Yuki's mother had had a *mon* . . . a family crest . . . which consisted of the tips of three pine trees on a mound. She had never been able to afford a formal silk crepe *kimono* with a crest, so she had taken comfort in the three pines in the yard. They symbolized her family tree . . . the long line of ancestors from whence she had come, as well as her descendants, who would grow straight, tall, and proud in this new land called America, to which she and her husband had emigrated as workers so long ago.

How tall the three trees must be after so many years! Yuki could hardly wait to see them again.

Next Yuki lingered over the memory of the orange tree in one corner of the yard. There were perhaps a dozen orange trees surrounding the house; they spread the almost overpowering scent of orange blossoms in spring and hung hundreds of golden balls in summer. But the tree in the flower garden, near her mother's bedroom, bore the sweetest fruit, and Yuki was forever climbing the tree, instead of using a sturdy bamboo pole with a bag and bent hook to pull down a fruit. The oranges tasted so much better, perched high up on a tree limb. Was she still nimble enough to climb that orange tree, after so many years?

The large garage adjoining the house was where most of the family's activities had taken place. The house was for sleeping; the garage was for talk-story, planning, laughing, games, work . . . actions that filled one's life.

Inside the house was the parlor . . . one never called it the living-room, since it was not a room for living. Here was the abode of the Buddhist god, ensconced in an altar which contained a brass pot for incense, a candle stand, fresh flowers daily, and an offering of freshly cooked rice. There was an all-important gong to call the gods to attention, or maybe to alert oneself that these were moments to exercise one's spirituality, one's relationship to God.

The whole family came together after dinner for prayers. There was a feeling of security, of serenity, that Yuki hoped to regain by sitting in the "parlor" once again. Would those renting the home allow her to do that? She would ask. There was no harm in asking. Just to sit where the altar had been, and the family had sat on fat cushions. She would let the love and closeness that had been in that house envelop her until they soothed her troubled heart and mind, and brought her the peace she had had as a youngster.

She glanced at Jeffrey across the room, plainly visible in the light of the moon. He was now fast asleep, and his deep, even breathing assured Yuki he would be rested for the long drive to her "home."

After that visit would come another visit . . . this time to Jeffrey's mother in the nursing home, the reason for which they had returned to Hawaii. Yuki had lived with Mother after her marriage, and they had grown close. But after she and Jeffrey had moved to California, they had had little personal contact with Mother, except through telephone calls, letters, and gifts. In the past few years, the nurses had refused their calls saying their mother could not come to the phone.

Would Yuki and Jeffrey be able to convey to Mother how concerned they had been about her? The mother who, although an immigrant and not understanding the English language well, had worked and saved enough to send both Jeffrey and Wade to the mainland universities of their choice? Engineering jobs had been scarce in Hawaii, so the two sons had had to move to the mainland. Their mother, however, had said her friends were all in Hawaii, and had refused to move to California. She preferred remaining in the old home, where the children had been born and raised, where she had lived for forty or more years. So Jeffrey and Wade had sent her monthly allowances which, now that she was in a nursing home, were more than they could afford. Definitely, they would have to take her home with them. She could live six months with Jeffrey, the other six months with Wade in Seattle. Yuki felt some relief that this action was the only one left, and soon she too fell asleep.

The long drive to the homestead where she had been born brought back many memories of past drives on the same two-lane road. Long stretches of black lava gave way to green meadows and hills, dotted with cows continuously munching on grass; eucalyptus stands lined the short stretch of four-lane highway. As they neared the homestead community, red-roofed cottages peeked from lush shrubbery and even the smell of yellow and white ginger was so familiar, Yuki knew she was finally going home again.

The driveway leading to "home" was not really a driveway. It was a steep and rocky road where stones rattled under the car as tires gripped fist-sized rocks and pebbles as best they could. But once at the top . . . ah, Yuki knew what peace and beauty awaited her.

When Yuki opened the door of the car in the parking area, she could hardly believe what she saw. Dried grass, three feet tall, surrounded the house. The unkempt yard swarmed with roosters . . . colorful, small, wiry, and saucy, weaving in and out of the tall grass, unafraid of people. They looked like fighting cocks in their stance.

As Yuki walked to the verandah, she saw the chickens had perched

anywhere and everywhere—perhaps for months and even for years—
and had left their droppings all over the porch where Yuki and her
family had spent so many evenings, as twilight moved into night and
stars popped out in ever greater numbers. The five steps leading to
the verandah were rotting, and Yuki was afraid the boards would
give way under her weight, or she might slip because of the slime and
mildew. A peek through a livingroom window showed junk piled all
over the room. There were stained cardboard boxes, old clothes,
moldy army blankets, soiled mattresses, rusted tools, and kitchen
appliances. What kind of people lived here anyway?

She glanced into the garage where her family had spent so many
working hours. Now the building was overgrown with vines, which
threatened to bring the whole structure down, for the vines had inter-
woven into a canopy a foot thick. There were two cars, covered with
dust and with flat tires and doors missing. Only inactive, useless
things were in the once-alive garage that had hummed with so much
activity!

Moss covered the house roof, and the gutters had not been cleaned
of leaves . . . since when? She remembered how each year, she and
her brothers had swept the zinc roof clean and scraped the gutters so
that the rain water would flow swiftly to the garden below.

The garden! Yuki moved swiftly to the three pines. Why, what had
happened to the tall, straight trees? They were not there anymore.
But when she neared the spot, she saw three pine trunks about three
feet tall, hidden by timothy grass. The tops had collapsed and rotted
in the grass, but new shoots were springing from the side of the
trunks, valiantly fighting to keep themselves alive despite years, even
decades, of neglect.

Instead of comfort, of peace, "home" brought pain, disillusion-
ment. Her birthplace had been desecrated beyond her imagination.
How could her relatives have had this happen? Why did they rent the
house to just anyone, especially people who would treat a home as a
rubbish dump? Or had the house been abandoned? Yuki jumped into
the car, and Jeffrey wordlessly started the engine and bumped down
the stony driveway.

"You can't go home again, can you?" she said to herself. "Things don't remain the same. Life goes on. We can't return to the past and expect to become a protected little child again." She did not cry. Her anger was stronger than her sorrow.

It was about an hour's drive from the old "home" to another home . . . the institution where Jeffrey's mother was being cared for. By that time, some of Yuki's composure had returned and she wondered, "Would Jeffrey succeed in getting Mother to come to live with them in California? What if she still refused to leave Hawaii? What if she said she would miss the weekly visits of old church and family friends— could they blame her for not wanting to leave an island where she had spent almost all of her life? Would it be difficult to care for someone on her way to senility? But didn't everyone forget things? Yuki herself often forgot names; she would remember them five or ten minutes later, when the need was no longer there. Sometimes she would search every room for her glasses, only to find them hooked over her head. No, it was no big thing, that her mother-in-law was getting senile. They could all get along with patience, compassion, and love. They could do things together at home. Maybe Yuki could even write down some of Mother's early experiences in Hawaii, early recollections of how things had been, so that Darlene's children and grandchildren could learn more about Great-grandma's early life in a foreign country.

They reached the nursing home and were admitted to the reception desk where they asked for Mrs. Masuda. The aide registered them, then took them to the diningroom and pointed to a woman sitting in a corner, being fed by a nurse. But that was not Mother. Definitely, it was not Mother. It was another woman with the same name. They checked with the receptionist.

"Mrs. Haruyo Masuda? That's she. Is something wrong?"

The woman's false teeth had been removed, so that her chin almost met her nose. The grey hair had been trimmed short into a serviceman's crew cut. The faded wrap was several sizes too big for the thin body. She stared into space, stiff, distrustful, unblinking.

When a spoonful of what appeared to be mush was pressed against the woman's lips, she opened her mouth and swallowed the food. Otherwise, she remained closed, defensive. Jeffrey and Yuki stood before her, unable to grasp what had happened to her. The woman would not or could not look at them. Was this really Mother?

"*Okaa-san*, Mother, it's Jeffrey. And Yuki. Don't you remember us?" Yuki whispered.

There was no recognition, no indication she had heard Yuki.

"*Okaa-san*, it's Jeffrey and Yuki. It's been a long time, hasn't it?" Yuki spoke loudly, and her voice echoed in the diningroom but no one even bothered to look at her. The mother continued to stare into space.

"Nurse, is my mother deaf?"

"Deaf? No . . ."

"How come she doesn't hear us? We know she's getting senile, but surely she can recognize us . . ."

"Senile? Weren't you told? Your mother has Alzheimer's. At this advanced stage of the illness, she doesn't recognize anyone. Or we think she doesn't. She hasn't been able to talk for several years, except for occasional grunts. In fact, at this point, we don't think she hears words with meaning, only sounds from us. She still responds a little to touch and she can walk if we hold on to her . . ."

"Alzheimers? Alzheimers! Nurse, my brother told me she was getting senile and she could receive better care in a nursing home. He never told me . . . he never told me . . . why didn't you people tell me what was happening?"

"I'm sorry . . . I'm truly sorry. But that's not our responsibility. It's not the nursing home's responsibility to be in touch with all of our residents' families. That's up to the doctor and the family member who is responsible for her. The doctor placed her in this facility at the family's request and with the family's consent. Our records are always open to the family. Why don't you check at the office?"

"Alzheimers! My brother . . . why didn't he tell me the truth? He knew, didn't he?"

"Of course. Aren't you in close touch with your brother?"

"Well, he lives in Seattle and I live in Los Angeles. We talk to each other on the phone, about Mother, but he never told me she had Alzheimers . . . only that she was senile and needed a lot of care."

"Sorry . . . it's always a shock, when one first hears the news . . ."

Jeffrey clenched his fist and pounded his knees angrily. "If I had known . . . if I had only known . . . there are so many things I wanted to tell Mother . . . so many things . . . and now it is too late . . ."

"Excuse me," the nurse said, and disappeared. Soon an aide came and resumed the feeding.

"I wanted to tell Mother 'thank you' for ironing my ROTC uniform every Sunday, while I was in high school," Jeffrey told Yuki. "She starched and ironed that uniform until it could almost stand up by itself. How many times I wanted to say 'thank you' but I felt awkward . . . embarrassed . . . to express my feelings. I wanted to say 'thank you' for buying me a clarinet when I was an eighth grader, and we couldn't afford it. She must have sold something of hers . . . a *kimono*, or something . . . but she got me this clarinet . . . a secondhand clarinet . . . the most precious thing in my life during those years. There is so much I wanted to thank her for . . . Mother! Mother! Listen to me . . . please! . . ."

The aide continued feeding the woman who still stared into space, like a scrawny metal robot.

Yuki and Jeffrey escaped to a secluded garden bench and hugged each other, crying.

"Yuki, we're too late. That is not Mother. Mother's gone. This woman, she's not Mother."

"Let's take her home back to California. I know I can take care of her . . ."

"Would that be fair to you? And to Darlene?"

"We'd be able to handle it. Why must Mother live the way she is now? She used to be strong, so independent. Look at her, Jeffrey. Please, let's take her away from here. Let her live a month with us, a week, even a day. Let's put her teeth back, give her a permanent, a dress that fits. Let's talk to her and talk to her and who knows, she might respond . . ."

They went back into the dining area. His mother was staring into nothing, her arms folded tightly across her chest, her mouth clamped shut. Only when the spoon touched her lips, even without food, did she open her mouth. Looking at her, they both realized it was too late.

They walked to the car, forgetting to say goodbye to the nurses and office staff. They drove for half an hour in silence. Suddenly, Jeffrey said, "Mother was happy while we were growing up. She was so proud when we brought home our report cards. When I became a captain in our school's ROTC, she polished and polished my bars until they shone. Then my brother and I both became engineers. As soon as we began working, we sent her all the money she needed and more. She had over sixty good years. What are five or even ten years of being a nobody, as compared to sixty years of a full, rich life? No, Mother wouldn't want us to pity her. The person we saw today is not Mother. Mother doesn't live in a nursing home. She lives in our hearts. Let's remember her that way . . ."

They drove for another half an hour, when Jeffrey suddenly pulled into a dirt road, put his head on the steering wheel and sobbed noiselessly.

"Why, Yuki, why? Why Mother? And why wasn't I told earlier? Why did Wade not tell me the truth? Who is he, God? That he thinks he is the one to make such decisions . . . that I should know or not?"

All Yuki could do was to put an arm over his shoulders and wait.

"What was it like, I wonder, that week . . . that day . . . when she slipped from being Mrs. Masuda to being a nameless human being, known by others but nameless to herself. Having stolen from her all memory of family and friends . . . one by one . . . of past and present. And we were not there, when she finally had to let go. I know Mother. I know she fought the disease. But by that time, she couldn't even remember or know how to call us to whisper, 'Help me. Please help me! Don't let them take me away from you. I'm frightened. I'm scared. Help! Please help!'

"At what moment did she say goodbye to the world as she knew it? Was it while she was eating with friends, and she paused to photograph their faces in her mind's eye? Was it at midnight, when our living room clock's chime woke her and allowed her to savor one last moment of comprehension, of familiarity with sounds and surroundings?

"And what were we doing? Why didn't we hear her desperate call? Maybe we were too busy complaining about how hard we had to work to pay her bills. We weren't even thinking of her . . . we were thinking of how we ourselves were being deprived of material things. And now it's too late . . . too late . . ."

They drove for another fifteen minutes, when Jeffrey said, "Yuki, let's borrow some money on the house so Darlene can attend Stanford. Mother worked hard to allow Wade and me to attend the universities of our choice. Now let's allow Darlene to go to the university of her choice. How proud Mother would have been, had she known Darlene had been offered a full scholarship to a prestigious university such as Stanford."

"And how will we pay for the nursing home?"

"We have to sign those papers Wade once sent us. From Social Services . . ."

"So Mother will be a charity case, living on Welfare. . . ?"

"This isn't charity. I've worked all these years and part of my salary has gone into taxes to provide for people like Mother and others. That's the way we do it now. It's no disgrace. There's no shame. It's not like the old days in Japan when each family had to look out for its own."

"Everything changes, doesn't it?" Yuki said. "Today, even the Japanese can send their parents to institutions. And we can't go home again, can we? Home is not the place it used to be."

"Maybe we're wrong," Jeffrey said. "Maybe the home you grew up in, that's not 'home.' That was your parents' home . . . while they lived there. We think of home as a place of security and comfort, because that's what our parents wanted to give us . . . a place we could be safe in. But our home . . . your home and my home . . . isn't that where we live? Isn't it the place where we should give security and comfort to our own children . . . to Darlene?"

Poor Darlene . . . she had been forced to sacrifice, too. To do without, to work after school. "We hardly ever talked to her, we were so busy with our double jobs. Only because Darlene is Darlene did she understand why we never had time enough for her."

It was difficult for Yuki to accept leaving her mother-in-law in the nursing home, as she had primed herself for so long to taking care of her at home. The three of them . . . she, Jeffrey, and Darlene . . . had agreed as to which room would be for Mother, because there was an attached bathroom. They had changed their dishes to light plastics, so Mother would not drop a plate or glass and hurt herself. Yuki had stocked up on Pampers, since Mother was surely bound to be incontinent at times. They had had a lock and key installed at the front gate so Mother would not go wandering about in a strange city. Every detail had been carefully thought out so that Mother would be comfortable and safe.

But the woman at the nursing home was not Mother. That woman could not recognize Jeffrey, her own son. Jeffrey and Wade had done what they could for her. They had gone without, so Mother . . . while she was still Mother . . . could have the best of care.

Yuki took a deep breath and exhaled . . . exhaled some of the misery, uncertainty, and fear of the past ten years. Breathe deeply, she told herself. Breathe away unacknowledged resentment, that your life, your actions, your activities were dictated by someone other than you.

She took another deep breath and exhaled the nostalgia of her birthplace she had stored and nurtured within herself, which was, she acknowledged, only memories enhanced by time. Breathe away all yearnings for a carefree, unfettered, protected life where responsibility was shouldered by others.

She took still another deep breath . . . yes, it was no disgrace, having the State of Hawaii and the Feds take care of her mother-in-law. Breathe away the idea that an imported cultural belief would have to be perpetuated forever, even though conditions had changed. Breathe away the belief that family members were the only ones responsible for another human being. This nation was one of cooperative assistance to the old, the weak, the poor, the ill, even to the unborn child.

Yuki had been outwardly uncomplaining all these years. But she had harbored resentment, bitterness, indignation, even as she was expressing concern. Let the resentment go . . . let the bitterness go . . . she was ashamed of herself.

The sight of her mother-in-law had shocked her. It would not be easy to forget that thin, frail body in its defensive stance, the unblinking eyes, the sparce grey crew-cut hair. But on the other hand, she remembered her mother-in-law smiling and waving at the airport . . . was it over thirty years ago? . . . when she and Jeffrey had left for California and their new jobs loaded with leis and macadamia nuts. One memory was of her mother-in-law; the other was of a body that had once housed her mother-in-law.

"Goodbye, Mother. Goodbye, home," she whispered, her head turned toward the window so Jeffrey would not see her tears.

The red-roofed cottages squatting within lush shrubbery exuded peace. The eucalyptus trees stood at attention . . . tall, silent sentinels bidding them farewell. And a mist crept slowly over the green hills and meadows of a ranch and spread a gentle white blanket over the cows still munching grass without a care in the world. Soon dusk also covered the sharp and jagged lava surrounding the airport area with an equally gentle but velvety dark blanket. The whole island was ready for a period of slumber and rest.

Yuki opened her arms wide, exposing her heart to herself, and releasing her senses of sight, sound, smell, and feeling to taste the outside world. Why, the multicolored bougainvilleas surrounding the airport were simply gorgeous. Why hadn't she noticed them before?

"Let's go home," Jeffrey said.

"Yes, let's go home," Yuki agreed, even as she acknowledged to herself that this island with all its heartaches and memories would also forever be "home" to her.

* 12 *

Two Artists

Flying from Honolulu, Oahu, to Hilo, Hawaii, the Big Island, we can glimpse the rugged Hamakua coastline between Honokaa and Hilo. Steep cliffs fight off crashing waves. At frequent intervals in the sugarcane fields, melted snow from Mauna Kea has formed streams and waterfalls that eat their way down deep gullies and gulches to the sea. The brown water turns clear as it flirts with lush bamboo forests on the valley floor, loiters near mango groves, and gently teases creeping *honohono* at the river's edge. Finally, the water merges with the ocean with little telltale signs of its long, often spectacular journey from Mauna Kea to the Pacific Ocean.

A short distance from these cliffs perch red-roofed plantation villages with exotic names: Laupahoehoe, Paauilo, Papaikou, Paauhau and Pepeekeo. It was to these sugar plantation camps that the early Japanese immigrants came, beginning in 1885. Japanese women were evidently not considered too highly, for they were paid $6 to $9 a month for working ten hours a day, six days a week.

Yet within a generation many women were to show that being Japanese or being a woman in Hawaii did not prevent a person from attaining leadership roles or from contributing to the community, nation, and even the world.

Two daughters of immigrants who captured and translated Hawaii's beauty, warmth, and strength into art forms are Alice Kagawa Parrott and Toshiko Takaezu.

Alice Kagawa Parrott

In Santa Fe, New Mexico, an earth-toned city hardly visible from the air because the adobe architecture merges with the desert and mesas surrounding it, lives a Hawaii woman who was born in Kalihi, close to where the billowing blue tapestry of the Pacific meets the *kukui*-forested velvet of the valley, hemstitched by silky, sandy beaches.

Hawaii's multicultural and multiracial environment produced a daughter of Japanese immigrants. She married Allen Morgan Parrott, a French-English-Welsh curator of an international folk-art museum, and adopted Ben, a Spanish Indian, and Tim, an American Indian. They live with Little Ben, a huge but gentle German shepherd; an Aracana chicken that lays eggs with green shells; and Cuate, a sixteen-year-old deaf dog with appealing eyes and stiff arthritic legs.

Alice grew up watching her parents celebrate New Year's Day by giving thanks to Earth-Nature spirits. In Santa Fe, Alice also offers thanks to spirits in and around her own home. All things, she believes, animate and inanimate, have a spirit of their own and should be respected. This is the Shinto way of life in old Hawaii and in Japan; this is also the Indian way of life in Santa Fe . . . to respect all things in nature and to give thanks for them. Most Indian art is a song of praise to the Earth which nurtures and sustains humankind.

Alice has synthesized experiences in her life and recreated them into artworks that are recognized as transcending a person's life; her weavings are said to have a life of their own, a life that speaks to and engenders response from people of many nations.

Visit tongue-twisting Nordenfjeldske Kunstindustri Museum in Trondheim, Norway, or the Victoria and Albert Museum in London, England; these prestigious museums display weavings done by this Kalihi woman born to immigrant parents and one of ten brothers and sisters. The parents came to till the soil and learned to work in red and black dirt, brown loam and grey cinder which centuries ago had spewed from the center of the earth in fiery splendor.

Alice, too, lives close to the life-giving earth. She derives much of her color for her weavings from Nature: indigo leaves, onion skin, marigolds, "madder," and cochineal . . . a tiny red insect that looks like a mealy-bug and feeds on cactus. From these products, Alice produces colors of burnt orange, rust, red, terra cotta, and other warm tones.

It seems strangely symbolic that of all the towns and cities in the United States, Alice selected Santa Fe to be her home. For Santa Fe is the city where, during the endless months of World War II, Japanese aliens from Hawaii were herded from other internment camps located throughout the country to await parole or to be returned to their homes in Hawaii. These internees had not been charged with any crime, but they were aliens in a land that would not allow them to become citizens, although many had lived in Hawaii for over forty years. In Santa Fe, they lived in a desolate stretch of desert . . . these doctors, dentists, fishermen, priests, Japanese school principals and teachers, businessmen, and even a bewildered beekeeper from the tiny privately owned isle of Niihau. And somehow, in this land of burning golden sunsets and freezing moonlit nights, the bitterness of these men, held prisoners for four long years behind barbed wire fences, disintegrated bit by bit, as the feeling of Oneness enveloped them . . . especially when they saw millions of desert flowers bloom at their feet after even a brief shower, and millions of stars mirrored the same beauty above them, like tiny white daisies strewn in God's path.

In a weaving called Fiesta—a celebration, a festival of thanksgiving and of praise—Alice has woven half a warm sun on a rich, earth-brown background. Two bands of blue run through the weaving, like slivers of sea and sky, and bound within these two strands of blue are many irregular squares of reds, oranges, mauve, yellow and other shades, together yet each distinct within itself. It is almost as if all nations have finally come together, and there is a fiesta, a festival, to celebrate the coming together of sun, earth, sea and sky and all its people into a harmonious whole.

Another weaving, Sea and Shoreline, is made of wool and linen in ocean blues, earth browns, pale greens, and gold. It is a portion of sea and beach caught in a moment of time, to be called forth during times of sadness and times of happiness. It is a promise and an assurance that beauty and serenity exist.

Toshiko Takaezu

Toshiko Takaezu is another Japanese woman artist who transcended race, sex, and other "artificial" categories.

In Bangkok, Thailand, and in nineteen states in the United States, public collections in museums include pottery made by Toshiko. The name on a card tacked near the pottery means little to viewers. They see the product, not the ceramicist. They care little whether it was made by a man or woman; Asian, Black, or Caucasian; a citizen or an alien. It is the product they see that impresses them: the colors, shape, harmony of parts, texture.

Toshiko's parents were immigrant laborers who worked on a sugar plantation, and Toshiko was born in one of the red-roofed plantation homes perched on a hill above the steep cliffs of Pepeekeo. One of eleven children, she grew up in what were always Depression years, when there are so many children existing on a plantation worker's wages. Under those circumstances, Toshiko had to be both independent and creative in meeting life's situations.

When Toshiko studied at the University of Hawaii, she enrolled in a class taught by Professor Claude Horan. Classes were held in a World War II quonset hut, which comprised the Ceramics Department. The building became a center of creativity, for Horan was open to new ideas. He set aside traditionalism and dogmatism and dared his students to see what would happen if they tried things differently.

Toshiko visited Japan in 1955, where she worked with a "Living Treasure" potter. She also visited Shoji Hamada, perhaps Japan's foremost potter. Both these men had demonstrated Horan's advice to go beyond all so-called rules of working with clay. Toshiko too was encouraged to explore the clay's possibilities. Observe, analyze, assimilate, interpret, develop something that transcends self with a being of its own; a good piece of art must be able to talk to people and tell them things without the artist being there.

"I am really fascinated with clay," Toshiko says. "It is alive and

responsive to touch and feeling. A piece usually starts with the crea-
tor's idea, but during the work process, the clay has much to say. Firing also contributes to the result. Potters do not have absolute control
over the products.

"In pottery, we need concentration in mind, strength in arms, skill
in hands, control of wheel, and ideas regarding harmony and
rhythm. We must listen to the voice of the material as it speaks to us."

Toshiko is one of only twelve recipients from 1959 to 1983 of a
prestigious Dickinson College Arts Award, which in the past included
poet Robert Frost, actress Judith Anderson, architect Eero Saarinen,
and the Philadelphia Orchestra. It is a rare and coveted honor to
receive this award. It is recognition of a symphony of body and soul
present in music, poetry, architecture, dance, pottery, and the theater,
among others. It is a national recognition of beauty that belongs to
the world and to future generations.

Toshiko will not sacrifice one type of beauty for another. "I use
elm, oak, other woods for firing," she explains. "I could use dogwood
as my back yard is full of them. But I wouldn't think of chopping
down those beautiful trees with pink and white blossoms and shiny
green leaves. If there is dead dogwood, I will use it, but I wouldn't cut
down a single live dogwood tree.

"When a pot is taken out of the kiln," she adds, "I never know what
to expect. There have been times when shimmering golds or tender
pinks have emerged unexpectedly, and I exclaim, 'How beautiful!' I
am not praising my own work. I am just amazed at the way the clay,
the glazes, and the heat in the kiln got together and produced the colors they did."

Despite her acclaim, Toshiko is down-to-earth, humorous. She
speaks softly as she works, sometimes to people around her, sometimes to the clay itself. "Pots should be visual and tactile, but they
should also be allowed to have sound, where possible. One day I accidentally dropped a small ball of clay in the pot before I sealed it. The
baked ball of clay makes little tinkling sounds when the pot is moved.

It seems the ball is communicating with the pot. The pot and the ball have little secrets of their own."

One can see Toshiko Takaezu is a poet as well as a potter.

Both Alice Kagawa Parrott and Toshiko Takaezu have transcended race and sex; they assimilated what they felt, loved, and believed in about Hawaii with its multifaceted society and interrelationships. They extracted the essence of Hawaii's character from their point of view and, using a selected medium, depicted through it their understanding and wonder of life and of their heritage.